The Most Inspiring Olympics Stories and Amazing Facts for Young Readers

A Motivational Gift Book for Sports Lovers, Athletes, Fans, Boys and Girls !

Harris Baker

Contents

Introduction	IV
Initiation to the Greatest Show on Earth!	
The Epic Olympic Adventure	4
Olympic Champions Stories	
Simone Biles	12
Michael Phelps	23
Noah Lyles	35
Katie Ledecky	44
Steph Curry	53
Lindsey Horan	62
Brittney Griner	71
Sydney McLaughlin-Levrone	80
Ryan Crouser	89
Scottie Scheffler	98
Amazing Facts, Records, and Moments	
The Evolution of Olympic Glory	112
Weird, Wild, and Wacky Olympic Moments	120
Olympic Legends	127
Olympic Legacy	133
Also by Harris Baker	136

Introduction

Welcome to The Epic Olympic Adventure!

Before we dive in, let's start with a quick glimpse of what's to come. In the first pages of this book, we'll dip our toes into the Olympic waters. What exactly are the Olympic Games? You'll learn about the fascinating origins of the Games and how they've grown into a global phenomenon. We'll also take a look at how the Games work, why cities compete to host the Games and more.

Next, we'll leap right into the stories of champions whose passion and grit have made them shine on the world's biggest stage. These athletes didn't start as superstars. They were kids with big dreams, just like you—facing obstacles, setbacks, and moments when they almost gave up. But through determination and hard work, they turned their dreams into reality. You'll meet swimming sensation Katie Ledecky, sprinting powerhouse Noah Lyles, and gymnastics marvel Simone Biles, along with basketball stars like Steph Curry and Lindsey Horan, and more incredible athletes who've made Olympic history.

Lastly, we'll get into some amazing Olympic facts, wild records, and incredible moments. We'll explore legendary athletes who paved the way for today's stars and discover how the Olympic legacy continues to inspire people around the globe.

Are you ready for an epic read? Let's go!

Copyright © 2024 by Harris BAKER

All rights reserved. No portion of this book may be reproduced in any form without written permission from the publisher or author except as permitted by U.S. copyright law.

Initiation to the Greatest Show on Earth!

The Epic Olympic Adventure

What exactly are the Olympic Games? Well, It's like the world's biggest sports party, where all the best athletes from every corner of the planet come together to compete in a mind-blowing variety of sports. We're talking swimming, gymnastics, running, basketball, and even snowboarding! The Olympics are so massive and prestigious that athletes train for years just for the chance to be there.

But did you know that the Olympics have roots going back thousands of years ? The original Olympic Games were held in ancient Greece (a civilization from long ago) nearly 3,000 years ago, starting in 776 B.C. (before the year zero)! They were part of a festival to honor the Greek god Zeus (the king of all the gods in Greek stories) and were held every four years in Olympia, a special place in southern Greece where the games were played. In their modern form, they've been around since 1896, when a Frenchman named Baron Pierre de Coubertin brought them back to promote peace and friendship among nations through sports. They're held every four years, bringing countries together in a huge and exciting event of sportsmanship, talent, and, yes, a whole lot of drama, excitement, and surprising victories.

The way it works is pretty cool. There are two types of Olympics: the Summer Games and the Winter Games. And here's where it gets clever. They take turns every two years. So, if you have the Summer Olympics in 2024, guess what's coming up in 2026? The Winter Olympics! Then, back to Summer in 2028, and the cycle goes on like this. But it wasn't always this way. Originally, both the Summer and Winter Games were held in the same year every four years. The Winter Olympics started in 1924 to feature sports played on snow and ice. Then, in 1994, they decided to alternate them every two years to give each its own spotlight.

What's the difference between these two? It's all about the climate. Summer sports like track and field, gymnastics, basketball, and swimming need warm weather or indoor arenas. Winter sports? We're talking snow and ice—skiing, figure skating, ice hockey, snowboarding. Imagine the Summer Olympics trying to include skiing in July! Yeah, not happening.

When it comes to the list of sports, it feels like there's something for everyone. In the Summer Games, you've got swimming races, basketball, gymnastics (Simone Biles, anyone?), soccer, cycling, and even stuff like skateboarding and surfing—yes, surfing! The Summer Olympics feature over 300 events in more than 30 sports. On the Winter side, you'll find events like ice hockey, ski jumping, snowboarding, and figure skating, where athletes do spins and jumps on ice that seem to defy gravity. The Winter Games may be smaller, but they pack in over 100 events across about 15 sports. New sports are sometimes added, and some are removed, keeping the Games fresh and exciting. So, no matter what kind of sport you're into, there's probably an Olympic event that will have you glued to the screen, biting your nails in suspense.

And here's the thing, this whole show is managed by one big organization, the International Olympic Committee (IOC). Founded in 1894 and based in Lausanne, Switzerland, these guys are like the puppeteers behind the scenes (people controlling everything but not seen), making sure everything runs smoothly, from organizing the competitions to making sure the athletes follow the rules. They work with National Olympic Committees from each country to coordinate everything. They're also the ones who choose where the Olympics are going to take place. Imagine a city like Tokyo, Paris, or Los Angeles has to apply, or "bid" (offer to host), to host the Games. They present these big fancy plans for stadiums, athlete accommodations (places where athletes will stay), transportation, and security, hoping the IOC will pick them. And when a city gets picked, it's like winning the lottery, but with a catch—huge responsibilities come along. The city has to be ready for the world to descend upon them (arrive in large numbers).

Hosting the Olympics can be both a blessing and a headache, meaning good and challenging. Sure, there's a ton of excitement and glory, and it can put a city on the map (make it famous) in a big way. But imagine the chaos of suddenly needing to build massive stadiums, manage thousands of athletes, and handle millions of spectators. It's like planning the biggest party in history while making sure everyone has a place to sit, something to eat, and a safe, fun time. Sometimes, this works out fantastically—places get new sports arenas, improved public transportation, and an economic boost (increase in money and jobs). Other times, not so much. Cities might overspend and struggle to make use of the huge facilities they built, turning them into "white elephants" big, expensive buildings that stay not used after the athletes and fans go home.

One of the coolest traditions of the Olympics, though, has to be the torch relay. This is when a flame, originally lit in Olympia, Greece (where the ancient Games began), is carried around the host country until it reaches the host city. The idea of the torch relay was introduced in 1936 during the Berlin Games. The torch symbolizes peace, friendship, and the light of spirit, connecting the ancient Games with the modern ones. People from different walks of life (different backgrounds), from famous athletes to everyday folks, carry the flame, passing it from one person to the next, sometimes traveling by foot, boat, airplane, or even into space! Yes, the flame has even been taken into space! And when it finally arrives? A huge cauldron (big metal bowl) is lit, marking the official start of the Games. It's like the world's most epic lighting ceremony.

Now, let me tell you, the Olympics really kick off in style with the Opening Ceremony. It's like the ultimate mash-up (combination) of sports, art, and culture, all in one jaw-dropping show. Fireworks light up the sky, dancers perform intricate routines, and musicians belt out tunes, all while showcasing the host country's unique traditions and history. Every host city pulls out all the stops (does everything possible) to make sure their ceremony is unforgettable. And one of the highlights? The Parade of Nations, where athletes from every participating country walk into the stadium, waving their flags and beaming with pride. Greece, because of its historical connection to the ancient Olympics, always leads the parade, and the host country comes last, basking in all the excitement and anticipation.

During the ceremony, there's also the Olympic Oath, where an athlete and an official from the host country pledge to compete and judge fairly, following the rules. The head of state of the host country then officially declares the Games open, and the Olympic flag is raised. It's a moment filled with tradition and significance.

But let's not forget about the Olympic Flame being lit. After the torch has been carried around the host country and handed off between hundreds of people, it finally reaches the stadium. This is the moment when the cauldron is set ablaze (lit on fire), and that fire stays lit for the entire duration (length of time) of the Games. It's not just a flame, though—it's a symbol of peace, unity, and the enduring, lasting spirit of the Olympics. It's the kind of moment that gives you goosebumps, knowing the Games have officially begun.

Once the competitions are over, we get the Closing Ceremony, which is like a grand farewell party. It's where the athletes, now friends and not just competitors, gather one last time. There's a festive vibe in the air, as everyone celebrates the end of this monumental event. The athletes no longer march in with their countries; instead, they come in together as one big global team, symbolizing how the Olympics bring people together. During the ceremony, the Olympic flag is lowered and handed over to the mayor of the next host city, a tradition known as the "Antwerp Ceremony" (named after the 1920 Antwerp Games where it first happened). Plus, the ceremony gives a nod to (acknowledges) the next host city, offering a sneak peek at what's to come in four years.

And let's talk about what every athlete dreams of—the Olympic medals. These gold, silver, and bronze medals are awarded to the top three athletes in each event, and they're not just shiny pieces of metal; they represent years of dedication, sacrifice, and hard work. Winning an Olympic medal is the ultimate symbol of achievement in sports. Fun fact: the "gold" medals aren't actually made entirely of gold—they're mostly silver with a thin layer of gold on the outside. In the ancient Olympics, instead of medals, winners received olive wreaths (circles made from olive branches) made from branches of the sacred olive tree. Another cool fact is that the design of the medals changes with each Games, often featuring artwork that reflects the culture and heritage of the host country. Still, they're worth a fortune in both sentimental (emotional) and historical value.

While we're on the topic of the athletes, did you know they all stay in a special place called the Olympic Village? This is like a giant, temporary home where athletes from all over the world live, eat, sleep, and hang out during the Games. The concept of the Olympic Village began in the 1932 Los Angeles Games to bring athletes together in one place. The Village is designed to make sure everyone is comfortable, with top-notch facilities (very high-quality buildings and services), food from different countries, and plenty of spaces to relax and meet fellow athletes. It's here that lifelong friendships are made, as athletes share experiences and bond over their love for sport, even if they don't speak the same language.

And if you've ever seen the Olympic flag, you know it has five interlocking rings (rings linked together)—blue, yellow, black, green, and red—on a white background. These rings represent the five inhabited continents of the world (Africa, the Americas, Asia, Europe, and Oceania (Australia and nearby islands)), and the fact that they're all linked together symbolizes how the Olympics unite people across the globe. The flag was designed by Pierre de Coubertin in 1913 and first flown in 1920. No matter where you're from, the Olympics are a reminder that we're all connected.

But more than medals, food, or ceremonies, what truly sets the Olympics apart are its values. The Games are built on the foundation (basic principles) of friendship, respect, and excellence. It's not just about winning—it's about showing up, giving your best, and competing with integrity (honesty and fairness). You see, the Olympics aren't just about personal fame; they're about bringing people together from different countries, cultures, and backgrounds. It's where athletes compete fiercely but also cheer for each other. After all, the struggle to reach the top is something everyone understands.

There's even a famous quote tied to the Olympic spirit that sums it all up perfectly: "The most important thing in the Olympic Games is not to win but to take part; just as the most important thing in life is not the triumph (victory) but the struggle (effort)." This Olympic Creed (statement of beliefs), written by Baron Pierre de Coubertin, reminds everyone that it's not just the victories that count, but the effort, dedication, and sportsmanship. It's a powerful message that encourages athletes to push their limits (try their hardest) but also to support each other, whether they win or lose.

And then, there's the Olympic Motto: "Citius, Altius, Fortius," which means "Faster, Higher, Stronger" in Latin (an ancient language). This motto was adopted in 1894 when the modern Olympics were founded. Recently updated to "Faster, Higher, Stronger—Together," the addition of "Together" highlights the growing importance of unity and working together in today's world. The Olympics are more than just a showcase of individual greatness or record-breaking achievements. They symbolize the unity and energy of the human spirit, bringing together one global community to uplift, inspire, and support each other in a shared celebration of human potential (what people can achieve).

The Olympic spirit of unity and collaboration shines brightly on the world stage, but it's built on the hard work and perseverance (not giving up) of the athletes themselves. Athletes train for years, competing in national and international events, all for a shot at qualifying (earning the right to participate) for the Games. Each sport has its own set of qualification rules, and not everyone makes the cut (meets the required standard). It's a grueling process (very difficult and tiring), and those who succeed often say it's like winning a medal in itself. Some athletes get there by winning at specific competitions, while others are chosen based on their world rankings. Either way, the road to the Olympics is paved with sweat, tears, and determination.

The Paralympics, which take place right after the Olympics, are another incredible display of athleticism. These Games are for athletes with disabilities (physical challenges), and they're just as intense and awe-inspiring as the Olympics. The first official Paralympic Games were held in 1960 in Rome. The word "Paralympics" comes from "parallel" Olympics, meaning they happen alongside the main Games. Athletes in the Paralympics push the boundaries of what's possible, they do more than people thought possible, showing that physical limitations are no barrier to greatness. In fact, the Paralympic Games have grown massively in both size and recognition, highlighting the strength and determination of these athletes.

And let's not forget about the Youth Olympic Games! This event, which started in 2010, is specifically for young athletes aged 15 to 18 who are looking to make their mark (become recognized) on the world stage. It's a bit different from the regular Olympics, as it combines sports competitions with cultural and educational activities, teaching the next generation of athletes about the values of sportsmanship and global citizenship (being responsible members of the world community). These young athletes are the future stars, and many go on to compete in the regular Olympics later in their careers.

With the Olympics' rich history and thrilling events fresh in your mind, it's time to meet the athletes who truly make the Games unforgettable. These modern champions, fueled by strong minds, teamwork, and perseverance, have pushed the boundaries of what's possible. Their stories are about rewriting what it means to compete on the world stage and changing how we think about international competition. Let's dive into their remarkable journeys!

Olympic Champions Stories

Simone Biles

"Never say never"
... The Gymnast Who Changed What's Possible

Imagine yourself as a wiggly little kid, full of wiggles and giggles, balancing on the edge of a curb—and then, whoosh! Life flips you like a pancake, leaving you wondering how to land. That's how it all began for Simone Biles. Born on March 14, 1997, in Columbus, Ohio, Simone's early life was anything but smooth cartwheels and confetti showers. Before she could even tie her shoes, Simone and her siblings had to move in with other families. This meant living with other families because their mother was unable to care for them, dealing with personal struggles that cast long shadows over their childhood. It was the kind of thing that could make any kid feel really sad and small. For Simone, those tough times were like bouncing on a trampoline—each bounce lifting her higher and higher. Every tough moment became like a hurdle she jumped over, showing a spirit as strong as the bars she'd one day swing on.

Now, here come the heroes of the story: Ron and Nellie, Simone's grandparents, swooping in like superheroes—no capes, just big hearts. They swooped in at just the right moment, stepped into the chaos and brought order. Ron, a retired U.S. Air Force veteran, and Nellie, a trained nurse with a nurturing spirit that could rival the sun's warmth, took in Simone and her sister Adria. For the two young girls, this indeed was a change in guardianship; but it was also a complete flip of their world. For Simone, Ron and Nellie were the kind of game-changers who rewrite entire stories, transforming her world in ways no one else could. They became Mom and Dad in every sense of the word. By 2003, the adoption was official, and Simone's life transformed from the uncertainty of foster care to the stability of a loving home in Spring, Texas. No more bouncing between foster homes; now Simone was flipping and laughing in a house filled with love and cartwheels.

Yet, life wasn't about to roll out the red carpet for her. At this point, Simone was still a little kid more focused on snacks than becoming the Greatest of All Time. But her carefree snack-and-play days didn't last long. When Simone was six years old, her life took an unexpected turn—a twist that would set her on a path unlike anything she could have imagined.

It all started on a seemingly ordinary day when Simone's daycare planned a field trip to a local gymnastics center. What started as an ordinary field trip turned into a magical moment—like finding a hidden room full of flips and tricks. As soon as she stepped into the gym, something clicked—like a key sliding perfectly into a lock. The gym was alive with movement, and Simone only had eyes for the flips and tricks happening all around her, she was spellbound, as if the gym held a secret magic meant just for her. She copied the gymnasts' moves with the excitement of a puppy chasing a ball, flipping and twisting like gravity didn't exist. Her raw talent shining so brightly it was impossible to miss. That someone was Coach Ronnie, who immediately saw the spark in young Simone. The gym sent a note home—like a golden ticket inviting her into a magical world of flips and fun. Instead of inviting her to a castle of magic, it invited her to tumbling classes, where Simone's adventure as a gymnast officially began.

From the moment Simone started tumbling, it was as if she had been flipping and twisting since the day she could crawl. Nellie, her ever-supportive mom, was by her side through it all. To Simone, Nellie was her cheerleader, confidante, and personal motivational coach. As she told once "She encourages me and never lets me feel down about something for too long." With Nellie's rock-solid support, Simone had the kind of foundation every child dreams of: someone to pick them up, dust them off, and cheer them on no matter what.

While Simone's life was filled with love and opportunity, life still had some tough moments in store. One of those came in August 2019, when her brother, Tevin, was arrested after a serious incident at a New Year's Eve party. It was the kind of news that feels like a storm cloud rolling in out of nowhere. But Simone, being her strong and determined self, didn't back down. She stood tall, even when it was hard. She shared a kind message online, sending love and sympathy to everyone affected. After a long legal process, in May 2021, Tevin was cleared of all charges because there wasn't enough evidence. Through all of it, Simone kept her balance, showing the world how strong she is both in her heart and on the mat.

See, even before Olympic gold was on the horizon, little Simone was already a powerhouse in the making. Her potential sparkled brighter than glitter at a birthday party, too dazzling to miss. Remember that first visit to the gym? It wasn't just a step onto a springboard—it felt like the perfect answer to all the hurdles Simone had already faced in life. The sense of wonder and possibility she felt that day marked the start of something incredible. Though no one could have guessed it at the time, this energetic, bouncy girl was about to create shockwaves in gymnastics, all thanks to a simple daycare field trip.

And so, this story has brought us here: Simone, adopted and deeply loved, discovering her destiny in the unlikeliest of places. This was only the beginning of a adventure as dynamic, twisty, and awe-inspiring as one of her jaw-dropping gymnastics routines. Her journey from her first flip to becoming a superstar gymnast—winning competitions like smashing candy-filled piñatas—is just getting started.

Alright, so by now, Simone Biles was that kid doing flips in the gym, the one that coaches started whispering about like, "Yeah, we might be looking at something big here." But let me take you back to the timeline for a second. After that fateful daycare field trip, Simone was all in. She officially started training at Bannon's Gymnastix with Coach Aimee Boorman, and if there was one thing that was clear early on, it's that Simone was a force. Like, by age 8, most of us were probably more concerned with whether our ice cream was about to melt, while Simone was out here conquering gym mats and perfecting backflips like it was no big deal. But hold on—because things really started to ramp up when she began competing. By 2007, at the ripe old age of 10, Simone entered the world of competitive gymnastics as a level 8 gymnast. In the gymnastics world, that's like strapping on a jetpack and launching into space. There are 10 levels in the USA Gymnastics Junior Olympics Program, so level 8 is already pretty high for someone that age (meaning she was competing at an advanced level usually reached by older gymnasts). Most of us were still trying to figure out long division by then, but Simone was already flipping, twisting, and turning like her muscles had a mind of their own. She was unstoppable, and you know what? That was just the warm-up.

Here's where things start getting serious. It was 2011, and Simone had already advanced to the junior elite level, which is where the best of the best in the country compete (the highest level for gymnasts under 16). This is the level that separates the "wow, she's good" kids from the "holy cow, she might take over the world" ones. At this point, Simone was more than a blip on the radar—she was a full-blown GPS signal. Her routines were the kind of jaw-dropping displays that made people go, "Wait, how did she do that?" Her coaches, her teammates, even random spectators—everyone knew she was special.

In 2011, Simone took her first significant steps toward national recognition by competing in the American Classic. Now, if you're picturing some casual local meet in a middle school gym, think again. This is a major competition where future Olympians get their start. And Simone? She didn't just show up—she owned the place. She won first in the vault and balance beam events and grabbed third in the all-around competition (which means she did well across all the different events combined). And let me remind you, we're talking about a 14-year-old girl in her early junior elite days already competing with the precision and cool-headedness of a seasoned pro. Simone wasn't here to play, folks. She was here to dominate.

So, naturally, the next year—2012—things got even more intense. Simone was racking up wins. She conquered the vault and the all-around competitions at major meets like the American Classic, the Alamo Classic, the Houston National Invitational, and the

Secret U.S. Classic (all important national competitions). She was collecting medals like kids collect Pokémon cards. And while most 15-year-olds were stressing over high school, Simone was out here flipping through the air with a level of intensity and focus that was on a whole different planet. Oh, and don't think she was doing it quietly either. Her routines were electrifying. Her power on the vault, her elegance on the beam (a narrow platform gymnasts perform on), her floor routines (dance and tumbling on a springy mat)—they all had that signature Simone Biles flair. You know—the kind that makes you want to hit the rewind button just to make sure you actually saw what you thought you saw.

But Simone's journey wasn't just about wowing crowds and stacking trophies. There was something deeper going on—a kind of internal fire that was pushing her toward greatness. At this point, her goal wasn't merely to be good at gymnastics; she was setting her sights on being the best. And I mean, like, best in the world level. And the thing is, when you're that committed, nothing—not even your own doubts—can stop you.

Enter 2013. This is where the story shifts into overdrive. Simone officially entered the senior elite level (for gymnasts aged 16 and over who can compete in the Olympics), which, in gymnastics terms, is basically like going from being a teenage superhero to full-on Avenger status. Senior elite gymnastics is where things get real. This is where Olympic dreams start to materialize, and where every gymnast is essentially competing for a spot on the world stage. It's cutthroat, high-stakes, and a level of intensity that most people would crumble under. But Simone stepped up to the plate like she'd been waiting for this her entire life, and she had...

In her first year as a senior elite gymnast, Simone took part in the 2013 U.S. P&G Championships, and let me tell you—she exploded onto the scene. She blew everyone out of the water, winning the all-around title like it was nothing. And remember, this was one of the biggest competitions of the year, and Simone, in her first year at the senior level, took home the top prize. But wait, that wasn't even the best part. Later that year, Simone did something that hadn't been done before. At the 2013 World Championships (an international competition where gymnasts from all over the world compete), she made history by becoming the first Black woman to win gold in the all-around event. Let's pause for a moment because that's no small feat. Think about what that represents—not just for Simone but for every young girl watching at home who thought maybe they couldn't reach that level, maybe they didn't have what it takes. Simone showed them, yes, they absolutely could. As she later explained in an interview with The Hollywood Reporter, that victory was bigger than just another medal. "I think it inspires a lot of the little girls out there to go in the gym and train harder," she said. And if that doesn't make you want to jump out of your chair and cheer, I don't know what will.

By this point, Simone was a bona fide gymnastics superstar. She was the name on everyone's lips. And she wasn't about to slow down either. Her historic 2013 World Championships victory was only the beginning. She spent 2014 continuing her domination, defending her U.S. and World titles in the all-around competition. At the 2014 Secret U.S. Classic, she cleaned house. She won gold in vault, floor exercise, balance beam, and of course, the all-around (winning in almost every event is a rare and amazing accomplishment). Simone's routines were starting to develop something of a signature—something uniquely "Biles"—and it was during her floor routines that one of her now-famous moves made its appearance: the double layout flip with a half-twist, a super hard move where she flips twice in the air while keeping her body straight and adds a half-twist at the end. And that was practically second nature for her.

Now, if you're wondering how someone at this stage in her career was handling the pressure, let me put it this way: Simone thrived on it. In 2015, she became the first woman to win her third consecutive World all-around title, which basically means she was now making history every time she stepped foot in the gym. With her third World all-around title under her belt, Simone had notched a total of 10 gold medals at international competitions, a record that was as mind-blowing as it was inspiring. And that's the thing about our girl—she was rewriting the entire gymnastics rulebook. She was setting new standards, for herself but also for the entire sport. Gymnasts everywhere started to look at her and think, "Well, if Simone can do it, maybe I can too." It was like she was pulling the entire world of gymnastics up with her, one gold medal at a time.

> THERE ARE FOUR MAIN EVENTS IN GYMNASTICS: VAULT, WHERE YOU RUN SUPER FAST, JUMP ON A SPRINGY BOARD, AND DO AWESOME FLIPS IN THE AIR BEFORE LANDING; UNEVEN BARS, WHERE YOU SWING AND FLIP BETWEEN TWO BARS AT DIFFERENT HEIGHTS; BALANCE BEAM, WHERE YOU CAREFULLY WALK ON A NARROW BAR, DOING FLIPS AND TRICKS WHILE TRYING TO STAY BALANCED AND NOT FALL OFF; AND FLOOR EXERCISE, WHERE YOU DO FUN FLIPS, JUMPS, AND DANCE MOVES ON A BIG SOFT MAT WITH MUSIC PLAYING.

But don't go thinking that Simone was all about perfection. She had her struggles too, both on and off the mat. In the midst of all the victories and records, she was still a human being. She still had moments of doubt, of frustration, of feeling like the weight of the world was on her (because, honestly, it kind of was). But through it all, she had something even stronger than her iron-clad routines—she had resilience. The kind of resilience that makes you keep going, keep pushing, even when it feels like everything is too much. And as we'd later find out, that resilience would become one of her greatest strengths.

But let's not get ahead of ourselves. Right now, we're still at the point in her story where Simone is climbing her way to the top of the gymnastics world, shattering expectations with every routine she performs. And the best part? She hadn't even hit the biggest stage of all yet. That was still to come. We're diving headfirst into Simone's legendary run at the 2016 Rio Olympics.

So, let's talk Rio 2016. By this point, Simone Biles was like a full-blown supernova, she was incredibly famous and shining brightly in the world of gymnastics. Everyone was super excited about her, and let me tell you, this was one of those rare times when the hype didn't even come close to the reality. Because when the Rio Olympics rolled around, she was the best. The 19-year-old gymnast from Spring, Texas, had the world's eyes glued to her every flip, twist, and landing. This was her stage, and boy, did she own it...

Let's start with the U.S. women's gymnastics team. They called themselves "The Final Five" (because they were the last team to have five members), and this group was a force of nature. Alongside Simone, there was Gabby Douglas, Aly Raisman, Laurie Hernandez, and Madison Kocian—a squad so packed with talent it was almost unfair. Together, they took on the team all-around competition and absolutely crushed it, winning gold for the United States. Simone's performances were, unsurprisingly, monumental. With jaw-dropping scores on vault, beam, and floor, she led her team to a commanding victory. But this was just the appetizer—because what Simone was about to do in the individual events was on a whole different level.

First up, the individual all-around—the big one. This is where gymnasts have to be near-perfect across all four apparatuses: vault, uneven bars, balance beam, and floor exercise. And Simone? She blew the competition away. She scored a total of 62.198 points. In gymnastics competitions, total scores usually hover around 57 to 60 points for top athletes. So scoring over 62 is like getting extra credit on an already perfect test—it's exceptionally high! But that's not all. She had a 2.1-point lead over the silver medalist, Aly Raisman. In gymnastics, athletes often win by tiny fractions, like tenths or even hundredths of a point. So a 2.1-point lead is like winning a race by a whole lap—it's a gigantic margin! It was the largest margin of victory in an Olympic all-around competition since 1980. And here's the kicker: Simone became the first woman in two decades to win both the Olympic all-around title and the World Championship all-around title in back-to-back years. Basically, she cemented herself as the best gymnast on the planet. No, scratch that—the best gymnast of all time.

But was she done yet? Guess what, not even close. In the individual events, Simone took home three more medals. She claimed gold in vault with an awe-inspiring score of 15.966. In gymnastics, routines are scored based on difficulty and execution. Scores usually range from 12 to 15 for excellent performances. So getting close to 16 means Simone performed an extremely difficult routine nearly perfectly! She blew everyone's minds with her explosive power and precision.

On floor exercise—her personal favorite—she lit up the crowd with another 15.966-point routine that included her now-iconic move, "The Biles" (a super difficult move where she does a double layout flip with a half twist). Again, scoring nearly 16 in floor exercise is outstanding and shows she's at the very top of the sport.

Then there was the balance beam, where she stumbled slightly and finished with a bronze (third place), but hey, even superheroes trip sometimes. In total, Simone walked away from Rio with five medals—four gold and one bronze. She joined an elite club of gymnasts like Larisa Latynina, Vera Caslavska, and Ecaterina Szabo, who also won four golds in a single Olympic Games. Not to mention, she became the first American woman to do so. That's a historic achievement!

Now, you'd think after an Olympic haul like that, Simone would slow down, right? hum, not exactly. After Rio, she took a well-deserved break in 2017 to recharge and let the world catch its breath. But when she returned to competition in 2018, she hadn't missed a beat. She swept the U.S. Gymnastics Championships, winning by a ridiculous 6.55 points. Remember how we said a 2-point lead is huge? Well, a 6.55-point lead is almost unheard of! In gymnastics, competitions are often decided by tiny margins, so winning by over 6 points showed she was in a league of her own—like winning a game by dozens of points.

And then she went on to win her fifth all-around title at the World Championships. Oh, and while she was at it, she also became the first gymnast to land a double-double dismount from the balance beam (which means she does two flips and two twists as she jumps off the beam) and the first woman to nail a triple-double on floor (that's three flips and two twists in one jump!). These moves are so difficult that most gymnasts wouldn't even attempt them, and she executed them flawlessly. At this point, she was rewriting the very code of gymnastics.

Then came the 2020 Tokyo Olympics—or, well, 2021. Everyone was expecting another Simone Biles masterclass, and for a moment, it seemed like she was ready to deliver. But something unexpected happened—something that shook not just the gymnastics world, but the entire global sports community.

During the team final, Simone decided to stop competing because she wasn't feeling right in her mind. She also had something called "the twisties," which means she got confused and lost her sense of where she was in the air while flipping and spinning. Imagine being in mid-air, doing one of those complex, gravity-defying twists Simone is known for, and suddenly losing all sense of where you are. It's terrifying—and dangerous. Her decision to prioritize her mental health over competition sparked a worldwide conversation about the pressures athletes face.

In her own words, "I say put mental health first. Because if you don't, you're not going to enjoy your sport, and you're not going to succeed as much as you want to." Team USA ended up taking silver (second place) in the team all-around, and Simone did return for the balance beam final, where she earned a bronze medal. This achievement was arguably as important as any of her golds. Why? Because it symbolized something bigger—her resilience, not just as an athlete, but as a human being. The gymnast who was once seen as invincible showed the world that even the greatest of all time can struggle—and still come back stronger.

After Tokyo, Simone took a two-year break from competition. It was time for her to heal, focus on her mental health, and decide what came next. And then came 2023. In what can only be described as the most epic comeback in gymnastics history, Simone returned to competition at the Core Hydration Classic. And like she always does, she didn't just return—she blew the competition away, winning the all-around title by an astonishing 5 points. Again, in gymnastics, winning by even 1 point is huge, so a 5-point lead is incredible! It showed that she was still miles ahead of the competition.

A few months later, she became the first gymnast ever to win eight national all-around titles at the U.S. Championships, all at the age of 26, making her the oldest woman to win the event. For context, gymnastics is often dominated by teenagers, so winning at 26 is a big deal. If anyone thought Simone was finished, she was more than happy to prove them wrong.

And that brings us to the 2024 Paris Olympics. It's the moment everyone had been waiting for—Simone Biles on the world stage once again. Would she be the same Simone that dazzled in Rio? Would the pressures of her past weigh her down? Well, Simone Biles doesn't get weighed down. She soars. The U.S. women's gymnastics team kicked off the Games by taking gold in the team all-around, marking the fourth time Team USA had won this event. Simone, of course, was a major contributor, posting top scores on vault and floor exercise.

Then came the individual all-around, where she made history again. Simone claimed her second Olympic all-around title, eight years after her first, defeating Brazil's Rebeca Andrade and her own teammate, Suni Lee. Winning multiple all-around golds is extremely rare; she's now one of only a handful of gymnasts ever to do it. This win put Simone in a league of her own. Then, during the vault final, Simone landed her signature move, the Biles, a double pike vault that's so difficult most gymnasts wouldn't even think of attempting it. It's a vault where she flips twice in a piked position (bent at the hips) without twisting. Performing this move successfully is like landing a trick shot in basketball from the opposite end of the court—it's that hard! And of course, she took home gold.

It was only during the balance beam final that Simone had an uncharacteristic fall and finished fifth. It was one of those rare moments where the world saw her as human again, but if you think that stopped her, think again. She bounced back in the floor exercise final to win silver, narrowly missing out on gold to Andrade.

With these four medals in Paris—three gold and one silver—Simone Biles became the most decorated U.S. gymnast in Olympic history with a total of 11 medals, surpassing all previous records. But perhaps even more remarkable than the medals themselves was what they represented: a redemption tour, a comeback story that defied all odds.

As Simone herself said after the Games, "I've accomplished way more than in my wildest dreams... A couple years ago, I didn't think I'd be back here at an Olympic Games, so competing and then walking away with four medals... I'm pretty proud of myself."

Simone left the door open for Los Angeles 2028, famously saying, "Never say never." And if there's one thing we've learned from watching Simone Biles flip her way through life, it's that she has a way of surprising us all—whether it's with her unparalleled skills or her incredible resilience. From that six-year-old kid on a daycare field trip to the most decorated gymnast in U.S. history, she's redefined what it means to be a champion in every sense of the word. And the best part? Her story's not over yet.

Michael Phelps

"Unstoppable"
... the most decorated Olympian of all times.

Have you ever been so full of energy that you couldn't sit still for more than two seconds? Or felt like your mind was racing so fast it might leave your body behind? That's what Michael Phelps, the most decorated Olympian of all time, was like as a kid. Born in 1985, in Baltimore, Maryland, he grew up in the Rodgers Forge neighborhood of Towson with an endless supply of energy that he simply couldn't contain. The adults in his life called it hyperactivity—being extremely active and having trouble staying still—but the truth was,

Michael was like a tiny human tornado, constantly moving, buzzing, spinning around in circles, doing anything to let off steam and energy.

He had two older sisters, Whitney and Hilary, who were both talented swimmers. Imagine growing up with siblings who could slice through water like sharks! They were so fast that the pool seemed like their natural home. It's no wonder Michael was eventually talked into the pool with them, even if he wasn't too sure about the whole "water" thing at first. In fact, young Michael was afraid to put his face underwater! Can you believe that? The same guy who would one day be known as the "Baltimore Bullet" and the "Flying Fish" started out too scared to even dip his head below the surface. His mom, Debbie, came up with a clever solution: she started him off with the backstroke—a swimming style where you float on your back and move your arms like windmills—so he could keep his face out of the water. Little did anyone know that this nervous little boy was meant by fate to become the greatest swimmer the world had ever seen.

Debbie was a school principal and a very strong and determined person. When Michael's kindergarten teacher said that her son would "never be able to focus on anything," she wasn't about to accept that. Debbie knew her son better than anyone and understood that his boundless energy didn't mean he couldn't concentrate; it just meant he needed a way to channel it—like directing his energy into something positive. She worked tirelessly to help him manage his focus and energy, especially once he was diagnosed with ADHD, a condition that makes it hard to focus and stay still, in sixth grade. She set up routines at home, kept an eye on his diet to avoid too much sugar (goodbye, candy bars!), and worked with his teachers to create special learning strategies that kept him engaged in school.

Michael's dad, Fred, was a police officer who works for the state of Maryland and a former athlete with dreams of playing football for the Washington Redskins back in the 1970s. Life took a different turn, and he ended up serving in law enforcement instead. Fred and Debbie separated when Michael was just nine years old, a split that hit him hard. For a long time, he had little contact with his dad, which added to the mix of emotions swirling inside him. Thankfully, his mother and sisters were there to support him through it all. His sisters became his first heroes, always leading the way with their swim practices and competitions. In their dedication and love for the sport, Michael saw a path he might someday follow—a small idea of what he wanted to do that grew brighter every time he watched them dive into the water.

Swimming, as it turned out, was the best thing that ever happened to Michael. He started at the age of seven, mostly because his mom thought it would be a good way to burn off some of that extra energy. She probably didn't expect him to take to it quite the way he did, though. Something about the rhythm of the water and the discipline of the strokes calmed him, almost like the pool was casting a spell over him. Patrick O'Connor, a professor in kinesiology—the study of body movement—would later say that "exercise can help control symptoms of ADHD by raising the baseline of dopamine," a chemical in the brain that helps with attention and feeling good. And it seemed to work wonders for Michael. The more he swam, the more focused he became. By the time he was 10, he was already breaking records for his age group in the 100-meter butterfly—a swimming race where you swim 100 meters using the butterfly stroke, which involves moving both arms together over your head while doing a dolphin-like kick—the same kid who started off scared of putting his face in the water was now speeding through it like a fast underwater missile.

So swimming was more than just a sport for Michael; it was therapy—something that helps you feel better and cope with problems. It gave him something to focus on, a goal to strive for. His family, especially his mom and sisters, made sure he knew they believed in him every stroke of the way. Debbie was more than supportive; she was fierce in her dedication to her son's dreams. Whenever a teacher or coach tried to say that Michael "couldn't" do something, she would respond with, "Well, what are you doing to help him?" It was her way of saying, "My son can do anything he sets his mind to, as long as he has the right people helping him along the way." That strong belief pushed Michael forward.

One of the most amazing things about Michael's early years was the way he and his mom developed their own secret language to help him manage his emotions. They created a special hand signal system that Debbie would use from the stands to help him stay calm and composed (in control) during competitions. If he was getting frustrated, Debbie would make a "C" shape with her hand, which meant "compose yourself." Just a small reminder, but enough to help Michael keep his cool and focus on what really mattered.

Michael's coach, Bob Bowman, entered the scene when Michael was just 11. Bowman saw in Michael what others sometimes missed—a fierce competitive spirit hidden behind his playful grin and boundless energy. To Bowman, Michael was like a diamond in the rough (someone with great potential who needs development), just waiting to be polished into something extraordinary. Bowman was known for being strict, almost like a drill sergeant—a very tough military trainer—and he quickly became a steady force in Michael's life, guiding him with discipline and high expectations. Under Bowman's watchful eye, Michael trained with unbreakable determination, willing to put in the grueling hours (very hard and tiring practice sessions) needed to reach the top. Michael would later say, "Training with Bob is the smartest thing I've ever done."

Bob was honing his mental game as well, believing that what separates elite athletes is their mindset. He introduced Michael to mental training techniques that would become pivotal in his career. One such technique was visualization. Every night, Michael would lie in bed and visualize himself swimming races perfectly, seeing every stroke from both his own perspective and from the stands. He would also imagine worst-case scenarios, like his goggles breaking or his suit ripping, planning exactly how he would handle them. Bob encouraged Michael to write down his goals—specific times he wanted to achieve in races—and keep them private, checking on them daily. This focus on the process over the outcome helped Michael develop an automatic resilience to "bad" performances, as he believed that as long as he trained properly and tried his best, he had succeeded. Bob's philosophy was that athletes perform better when they're relaxed and focused on the process, not the outcome, a lesson Michael embraced fully.

Outside of the pool, Michael was just like any other kid. He loved playing video games with his friends, goofing around, and eating his favorite foods (he was famous for his enormous appetite!). He found joy in simple things like spending time with his buddies, laughing at silly jokes, and enjoying family gatherings. These moments kept him grounded, helped him stay connected to what's important, and reminded him that life wasn't all about competition—it was also about friendships and fun.

It wasn't long before Bowman realized Michael had the potential to become an Olympic swimmer. When Michael heard that, he went all-in (he fully committed), giving it everything he had. He quit other sports like soccer, lacrosse—a team sport played with a small rubber ball and a long-handled stick—and baseball, focusing all his energy on swimming. The pool became his second home, and the dream of competing in the Olympics was the fire that kept him going. Even though things didn't always go perfectly—losing his first big competition was so frustrating for young Michael that he threw his goggles on the ground in a fit of anger. Coach Bowman warned him about his behavior, teaching him that it was just as important to accept losing without getting angry as it was to celebrate victory. "It's when your body is not in the best situation, your mind is not in the best situation, and things are against you—those are the times that really count," Bowman told him. Michael took that lesson to heart, learning to use his anger to work harder.

Michael's friendships with his teammates also played a significant role in his growth. He formed close bonds with fellow swimmers, sharing laughs during practice and supporting each other through tough training sessions. These friendships made the hard workouts more bearable and added joy to his journey. They weren't just teammates; they were like a second family, sharing the good and bad times of competitive swimming.

His first major setback (failure that makes things more difficult) came at the 1999 U.S. National Championships when he finished last in the 200-meter butterfly—a long-distance race using the butterfly stroke. For anyone else, this might have been enough to call it quits. But Michael, even at just 14, wasn't about to give up. Instead, he used that experience to make him train even harder, coming back even stronger at the 2000 U.S. Spring Nationals, where he placed third. Just a few months later, he qualified for the 2000 Summer Olympics in Sydney, Australia. He was only 15, the youngest male swimmer to represent the United States in an Olympic contest since 1932. Although he didn't win a medal in Sydney, finishing fifth in the 200-meter butterfly, the experience of being on the Olympic team at such a young age only made him even more determined.

The pool had transformed Michael in ways that no one could have predicted. From a little boy too scared to put his head underwater, he became a young athlete with big dreams, unbreakable focus, and a heart that refused to give up, no matter how tough things got. As he swam lap after lap, fueled by his family's unwavering support, his coach's persistent guidance, and his own dreams of Olympic gold, Michael Phelps was on his way to becoming a legend.

There he was—a teenage Michael Phelps, fresh off his first Olympics, where he finished fifth in the 200-meter butterfly. For most 15-year-olds, just making it to the Olympics would've been a "drop the mic" moment—an achievement so impressive that nothing more needs to be said. But Michael was only just getting started. That fifth-place finish wasn't the final achievement; it was a spark that ignited a fire in him, one that would only grow brighter and hotter. If anything, the 2000 Sydney Olympics confirmed what his coach, Bob Bowman, already knew: Michael wasn't a kid who was going to settle for "good enough." He wanted to be the best in the world, period.

Once they got back to Baltimore, Bowman ramped up the training like he was preparing Michael for an intergalactic swim battle. And if you're thinking this meant a few extra hours in the pool, think again. Michael swam every single day of the week—yes, even on Sundays, Christmas, Thanksgiving, and his birthday. Bob had a theory: if Michael trained every day, that would add over 50 more training days each year compared to his competitors. "They were always playing catch-up," Bowman would later say. While other swimmers got a day off here and there, Michael was in the water, arms slicing through the pool like he was born for it. This routine continued for over five years, a marathon of commitment and intensity that shaped him into a swimming machine.

Outside the pool, Michael found time to enjoy life as a teenager. He loved hanging out with friends, watching movies, and playing video games. These moments of relaxation were essential, giving him a break from the intense demands of training. He was known for his good humor and loved pulling pranks on his friends, showcasing a playful side that balanced his fierce competitiveness.

In 2001, just a few months after the Sydney Olympics, Michael became the youngest male swimmer in history to set a world record. He shattered the record in the 200-meter butterfly with a time of 1:54.92 at the U.S. Nationals in Austin, Texas. That means he swam 200 meters (about the length of two football fields) using the butterfly stroke faster than anyone ever had before! Imagine the headlines: a 15-year-old kid not only holding his own but actually taking down a world record. And if that wasn't wild enough, he would go on to break his own record several more times, each time pushing the boundaries of what was thought humanly possible. He was only fifteen years and nine months old, and already he was leaving his mark on the world stage.

As legendary as his accomplishments were, it wasn't all medals and world records. This was Michael Phelps, after all, and where there was water, there was also an endless, ferocious drive. He had a focus and ambition that could almost be called obsessive—Bowman would even compare his training approach to that of a drill sergeant. Michael would wake up before dawn, dive into the freezing cold water, and swim for hours. Then he'd take a break to lift weights, eat, maybe catch a nap, and go right back to the pool in the afternoon for more laps. His routine was so intense that even the concept of "hard work" seemed to fall short. "Eat, sleep, and swim," Michael once said. "That's all I can do." His daily life was like something out of a Rocky training montage—a series of scenes showing intense training—but with chlorine and goggles instead of boxing gloves and stairs.

As Michael kept breaking records and blowing people's minds, the world started comparing him to swimming legend Mark Spitz. In the 1972 Olympics, Spitz had won seven gold medals, a record that no one had even come close to since. Now, here was this tall, lanky teenager with a six-foot-seven wingspan—meaning his arms stretched out to six feet and seven inches (about 2 meters), longer than most people his height—and feet so big they were practically flippers, looking like he just might be the guy to take on Spitz's record. At first, Michael didn't quite understand why everyone kept mentioning Spitz's name. "Why are they asking me about Mark Spitz? What did he do?" he once asked his coach, baffled by the comparisons. But when Bowman explained who Spitz was and the legacy he'd left behind, Michael got it. Suddenly, he saw a new mountain to climb.

By 2003, the rivalry between the United States and Australia was heating up, especially in the world of swimming. The Australians had a superstar of their own, Ian Thorpe, known as the "Thorpedo." Thorpe was three years older than Michael and already a household name in Australia. He was fast, powerful, and his fans were convinced he was unbeatable. But Michael wasn't intimidated. At a special competition called the "Duel in the Pool," the U.S. team faced off against the Australians. Thorpe, unfortunately, was sidelined with a health issue, which meant the world had to wait a little longer to see the two titans go head-to-head. But the rivalry was there, simmering beneath the surface, and it would eventually turn into one of the greatest showdowns in swimming history.

Finally, the moment arrived at the 2003 World Championships in Barcelona. Phelps vs. Thorpe. America vs. Australia. It was the kind of matchup that sportswriters dream of. Michael was just 18, barely old enough to vote, and Thorpe was at the peak of his career. Yet, in race after race, Michael outperformed. He won five medals in Barcelona, set five new world records, and established his status as the rising star of competitive swimming. One of the most jaw-dropping moments came during the 100-meter butterfly semifinal, where he broke the world record with a speed that left the crowd stunned. In another race, the 200-meter individual medley—a race where you swim all four major strokes: butterfly, backstroke, breaststroke, and freestyle—he beat his own record yet again, finishing so far ahead of the pack that it looked like the rest of the swimmers were in slow motion.

And let's talk about his body for a second because it seemed custom-made for the pool. Standing at six-foot-four, Michael had the torso of someone even taller—around six-foot-eight—which gave him an insane reach advantage. His arms were so long they could wrap around a whale—and his size-14 feet acted like natural paddles. Add to that his double-jointed knees and elbows, which helped him perform his famous dolphin-like kick, and you had an athlete who was practically designed for swimming. "He flies across a pool like water is someone else's problem," wrote journalist Jody Berger. "He doesn't punch his way through the wet stuff but hydroplanes—skims over the surface—across its surface at a speed few humans can match." It was like watching a real-life superhero in action.

With all this momentum behind him, people started to wonder: could Michael be the next Mark Spitz? Then something remarkable happened. In late 2003, he signed a contract with Speedo (a company that makes swimwear)showed how much faith the company had in his potential. The contract promised him a $1 million bonus if he could match Spitz's record of seven gold medals at a single Olympics. One million dollars—for a teenager! And though Michael tried to stay humble, he couldn't deny that the challenge had lit a fire in him. He started thinking, Maybe I could actually do this.

But, as always, Michael kept his head in the game and tried not to get too carried away with the excitement. "If you get caught up in it, your mind will take over and control you," he told The New York Times. "I have to make sure I'm in control." Michael was fiercely protective of his focus and had developed his own ways of blocking out the noise. One of his favorite strategies was to listen to rap music before every race, a ritual that helped him stay pumped up and locked in. He'd blast tracks by Snoop Dogg, 50 Cent, and Eminem, letting the beats drown out everything else. "When I get out of the car, the last song stays in my head," he explained. "It's there all during practice, in my head." For Michael, those beats were like a secret weapon, a mental shield that helped him stay calm and fierce in the pool.

Michael also found joy in mentoring younger swimmers. He would often take time to encourage and share advice with up-and-coming athletes, emphasizing the importance of hard work and passion. These interactions not only helped others but also reminded Michael of how far he had come and the importance of giving back.

With the 2004 Olympics on the horizon, Michael threw himself into his training with even more intensity. Bob Bowman was relentless, pushing him to limits most people couldn't even imagine. But Michael embraced it all, day after day, lap after lap, visualizing each race in his mind. At night, he'd lie in bed, mentally going through every single stroke of every race, as if he could see himself from above, gliding through the water. He'd imagine best-case scenarios, where everything went perfectly, and worst-case scenarios, where something went wrong—like his goggles filling up with water. He was so prepared for any situation that when those things did happen—like they eventually would in Beijing—he'd know exactly how to respond.

By the time Michael arrived in Athens, he was no longer the nervous teenager from the Sydney Olympics. He was an 18-year-old phenomenon, ready to take on the world. The media couldn't get enough of him, and fans were eager to see if he could really do what no one else had done since Mark Spitz. Michael's dream was within reach, and everyone could feel it.

And then, finally, it was time for the 2004 Athens Olympics. This was the moment everyone had been waiting for—Michael Phelps, 18 years old, taking on the world with a goal so outrageous it almost sounded like a dare: seven gold medals. Seven chances to prove that he wasn't just another fast swimmer but a legend in the making. Yet, as ambitious as his goal was, Michael approached it with a cool head, saying, "One gold medal is all I want. You are a more recognizable, notable person with the gold medal. So one gold medal is my goal. And whatever happens after that, happens."

But of course, Michael being Michael, he didn't walk away with just one gold medal. Athens was his stage, and he excelled, winning six golds and two bronze medals—an achievement that was absolutely mind-blowing for an athlete his age. By the end of those Games, Michael had already broken records, becoming one of the most successful swimmers in a single Olympics since, well, Mark Spitz himself. He even won his final gold medal in the 4x100m medley relay—a team race where each swimmer does a different stroke—with a broken goggle that had filled up with water. But he'd visualized that exact worst-case scenario so many times that he didn't even flinch; he powered through, racing like he could see perfectly. For Michael, it was all about preparation. "Things won't go perfect," he said. "It's all about how you adapt from those things and learn from mistakes."

After Athens, the world officially knew Michael Phelps. He wasn't just a fast kid from Baltimore anymore; he was the face of competitive swimming. Even though he could've taken it easy, he went back to training with renewed drive. By 2008, with the Beijing Olympics on the horizon, Michael wasn't just aiming to match Mark Spitz's seven golds. No, this time he was thinking bigger. This time, he was gunning for eight.

Between competitions, Michael made sure to enjoy life. He traveled, met new people, and indulged in his hobbies like playing video games and watching his favorite TV shows. These activities helped him relax and recharge, ensuring he didn't burn out from the intense pressures of his sport. He also spent quality time with his family, strengthening the bonds that had supported him from the beginning.

The 2008 Beijing Olympics would be Michael's masterpiece. People called him the "Baltimore Bullet," the "Flying Fish," even a "machine." But even Michael couldn't have scripted a performance like the one he gave in Beijing. He competed in eight events over eight days, with barely any rest between races. The pressure was extremely high. Every time he climbed up on that starting block, the entire world held its breath, waiting to see if he could pull it off. And yet, race after race, he kept winning. Gold medal. Gold medal. Gold medal. By the time he reached his seventh event, he was tied with Spitz's record and poised for history. But here's the twist—the seventh race was the 100-meter butterfly, an event he barely won by a fraction of a second. To this day, that victory is remembered as one of the greatest races in Olympic history, with Michael touching the wall just 0.01 seconds ahead of the runner-up. "It was so close, I didn't even know if I'd won until I looked up at the scoreboard," he said. Can you imagine? In the time it takes to blink, he'd managed to keep his dream alive.

When Michael swam his final event, the 4x100-meter medley relay, he and his teammates set a new world record, bringing Michael's total to an unprecedented eight gold medals in a single Olympics. His victories were so spectacular that it seemed like he was on another planet, swimming at speeds no one had ever seen. "I want to test my maximum and see how much I can do," he'd said before the Games. In Beijing, he showed the world exactly what that meant.

After Beijing, you'd think Michael would have been satisfied, maybe even ready to retire with his historic eight-gold collection. But no, he went right back to the pool, training for the 2012 London Olympics. This time, however, things were different. Michael had been swimming competitively since he was 7 years old, and the intense schedule—the relentless training—it was all starting to wear him down. The fire that had fueled him for so long was flickering. He'd become a global icon, yes, but he was also struggling with something that wasn't visible in the pool: mental exhaustion (feeling very tired in his mind). Yet he pushed on, determined to give London everything he had.

In London, Michael didn't win eight golds, but he still did very well, taking home six medals—four golds and two silvers. While this might sound like a "lesser" performance compared to Beijing, it was anything but. With those wins, he became the most decorated Olympian of ALL TIMES, with a grand total of 22 medals. No one else had ever come close to that record. For Michael, it was a moment of both triumph and relief. He'd done it. He'd proven everything he set out to prove, and he was ready to step away from the pool.

After London, Michael announced his retirement, planning to focus on life outside the pool. He took up golf, spent time with his family, and worked on his mental health, which he'd struggled with throughout his career. In fact, he became a powerful advocate for mental health awareness, openly discussing his battles with depression (a serious condition that makes you feel very sad and hopeless) and helping to break the stigma surrounding athletes and mental health. He once said, "I like to just think of myself as a normal person who just has a passion, has a goal and a dream and goes out and does it. And that's really how I've always lived my life."

During this time, Michael reconnected with his father, Fred, mending a relationship that had been strained for years. This personal growth was significant, allowing him to find peace. He also married his longtime girlfriend, Nicole Johnson, and became a father, finding immense joy in his family life. Playing with his son, Boomer, brought out a new side of Michael—the playful dad who loved nothing more than making his child laugh.

Even in retirement, the pool kept calling him back. In 2014, after two years away, Michael came out of retirement, determined to give the Olympics one last shot. The Rio 2016 Games would be his final act, a swan song to end his career on his own terms. At 31, an age most competitive swimmers would consider "ancient," he made his comeback. "I want to be able to look back and say, 'I've done everything I can, and I was successful,'" he said. "I don't want to look back and say I should have done this or that."

In Rio, he wasn't the unstoppable force of 2008, but he was still a legend, still the Michael Phelps who could pull off miracles in the water. Imagine that: he won five new gold medals and one silver, adding to his already staggering medal count and bringing his total to 28 Olympic medals—23 of them gold. In his last individual race, the 200-meter butterfly, he reclaimed his title, proving that even after all those years, he was still the greatest.

After Rio, Michael retired for good. This time, it was final, and he knew it. He'd done everything he set out to do and more. He'd set world records, shattered expectations, and inspired millions around the world. His legacy was in the way he changed the sport of swimming forever. Through his foundation, he continued to promote water safety and mental wellness, giving back to the sport and community that had given him so much. And maybe that's what makes Michael Phelps a true legend. In his own words: "The more you dream, the farther you get." Michael Phelps dreamed big, swam hard, and changed the world one stroke at a time.

Noah Lyles

"Fast Through the Struggles" ... The Runner Who's Rewriting Speed Rules

Noah Lyles was born on a scorching summer day in Gainesville, Florida, where even the air felt like it could run a marathon. Back then, little did the world know that this tiny baby, swaddled in a hospital blanket, would grow up to be one of the fastest humans ever to set foot on the planet. But before any of that, there were dinosaurs to fight—or at least, in Noah's hyperactive imagination. With an endless burst of energy and legs that couldn't sit still, Noah had the heart of a sprinter before he could even walk properly.

Noah's parents, Kevin and Keisha, were no strangers to fast feet either. They had been sprinters too, racing down the track like human rockets during their college years at Seton Hall University (a college in New Jersey). Some families pass down heirlooms or funny stories, but Noah inherited speed. It ran in his blood like superhero powers, and like any good superhero origin story, young Noah had his fair share of battles. One of the earliest was asthma, a condition that makes it hard to breathe because your airways can become narrow and swollen. That sneaky villain had young Noah gasping for air like he'd been chased by a cheetah, and it was no fun at all. Imagine trying to keep up with the fastest kids on the playground when you're struggling to breathe!

When Noah was just a kid, he spent a lot of time in hospitals, hooked up to a nebulizer machine (a device that turns medicine into mist so you can breathe it into your lungs). That made strange whirring noises like a robot on its lunch break. His asthma was so severe that it seemed, at times, it would slow him down before he even got his start. But Noah wasn't the type to give up. At six years old, he had his tonsils and adenoids removed (small tissues in your throat and behind your nose that can sometimes cause breathing problems), which might not sound like the stuff of legends, but it made a huge difference for him. After that, breathing became a little easier, the air didn't feel so heavy, and he didn't need to visit the hospital as much. Score one for Team Noah!

Growing up in Alexandria, Virginia—because his family moved there when he was still a little tyke—Noah spent most of his days either in school or bounding around outside with his younger brother, Josephus. Josephus was fast too, and the two of them could've been the real-life versions of The Flash, racing down their neighborhood streets like their sneakers were on fire. Alexandria was practically the perfect place for two young speedsters to grow up. It had parks with wide open spaces where they could let their legs fly, and tracks where they would later chase each other in circles, daydreaming of Olympic gold medals.

Noah had more hurdles to jump over than he probably would've liked. He was homeschooled until the second grade, and once he started attending regular school, things got a bit tricky. It wasn't that Noah wasn't smart—his brain just worked a little differently. Teachers soon realized he had dyslexia and ADHD. ADHD is when your brain has trouble focusing or sitting still, and dyslexia is when it's harder to read because letters and words can get mixed up, but both just mean your brain works in a special way. This made sitting still in a classroom as difficult for Noah as running in flip-flops. Words sometimes played tricks on him, and his attention would zip away like a rocket. But this didn't stop Noah from doing what he loved—moving, running, jumping, and flipping like a little human whirlwind.

As a kid, he tried out gymnastics, a sport where flipping through the air like Spider-Man was totally normal. Gymnastics gave Noah a chance to release his crazy energy, and soon he was leaping and twirling like a pint-sized acrobat. But, like all great heroes, he found his true calling early on. At 12 years old, Noah found himself face-to-face with his destiny on a track, and when he felt the spring of the surface beneath his feet, it was like the universe whispered, "Run, Noah. Run fast." And my firend, did he ever listen. From then on, the Lyles boys, Noah and Josephus, were like lightning bolts—zipping through every track meet and neighborhood race they could find. Together, they chased each other down lanes like they were racing towards the future itself. But while Josephus was content to enjoy the moment, Noah had bigger plans. His dream wasn't just to be fast, but to be the fastest.

Noah's parents, wise to their boys' talent, supported their every sprint and leap, cheering them on from the sidelines. And sure, Noah had to work harder than a lot of other kids. His ADHD meant that focusing wasn't his strongest suit, but running gave him clarity. It was like every time his foot hit the track, the world slowed down just enough for him to think straight.

By high school, Noah's relationship with running was no longer a casual fling—it was a full-blown obsession, he was totally dedicated. There was something magical about how fast his legs could move, how the wind roared in his ears, and how everything else faded into a blur when he hit top speed. In school, Noah was busy thinking about his next race, imagining himself as a blur of lightning, faster than anyone else in the world.

Remember Josephus? They weren't only brothers—they were also rivals, teammates, and each other's biggest competition. The track in their neighborhood was basically a battleground where the Lyles brothers dueled it out, race after race. The air would sizzle with the crackling sound of their sneakers on the pavement as they chased each other, fueled by nothing but pure sibling rivalry. And trust me, Josephus was no slouch, he was really good too. He could keep up with Noah like nobody else could, pushing him to run faster, better, and stronger. It's like they were destined to be track stars, born into a family where speed was practically their last name.

Soon enough, Noah's talent spread far and wide. Coaches were whispering his name like it was a secret code to unlock the next big thing in track and field. "Lyles, that kid is special," they'd say. His high school, T.C. Williams (you know, the one from the movie "Remember the Titans"—no big deal), started to see that Noah was something else entirely. His sprinting was like watching a cheetah chase its prey, except this cheetah wore flashy shoes and had a style all his own.

At 17, Noah's golden moment arrived when he got the chance to compete at the 2014 Summer Youth Olympic Games in Nanjing, China. It was his first taste of real international competition—an arena filled with the fastest teenagers from around the globe, each one looking to claim victory. But here's the thing about Noah: he wasn't scared. He wasn't nervous. He was hungry. Hungry to prove that he belonged among the best, that he could stand at the starting line and blow past the competition. And that's exactly what he did. When Noah sprinted the 200 meters (that's half the length of a standard track), it was as if time itself bent around him. His legs pumped, his arms swung, and for 20.93 seconds (an incredibly fast time), the world held its breath. As he crossed the finish line, he was miles ahead of everyone else (it felt like that). The gold medal was his, and the world was put on notice: Noah Lyles was here, and he was fast. He wasn't just some kid from Virginia anymore; he was a Youth Olympic Champion. That gold medal was more than a metal hanging around his neck—it was a crown, a declaration that this kid was destined for greatness.

After that, Noah's star was burning so brightly, even the sun might have needed sunglasses to look at him (you got the idea). He didn't slow down, not for a second. High school races became easy pickings for him. He was like a shark in a pool of guppies, and every track meet felt like it was his for the taking. In 2015, during his junior year, he switched things up a bit and showed off another one of his hidden talents—the high jump. At a meet, he cleared an astounding 2.03 meters (that's over 6 and a half feet, by the way), as casually as if he were stepping over a puddle. Was there anything Noah couldn't do? At this point, it seemed like he could wake up one day and decide to break a world record in any sport, and nobody would be surprised.

But Noah wasn't done proving himself, not by a long shot. He had his eyes set on bigger, shinier prizes—because if there's one thing Noah loved more than winning, it was winning big.

In 2016, he went all out. That year, at the New Balance Nationals Indoor, Noah blew the roof off the place (metaphorically, of course) when he won the 200 meters with a time of 20.63 seconds. And then, because one victory clearly wasn't enough for this speed demon, he also crushed the Arcadia Invitational (a prestigious high school track meet) by winning both the 100 meters (the classic sprint race) and the 200 meters. His victories were piling up faster than homework before a long weekend, and his personal bests were getting even better. Noah's life was changing faster than the gears on a racing bike. His name was popping up in every track and field conversation like confetti at a birthday party. But despite all the attention and medals, Noah kept his cool. He wasn't arrogant, just confident—he knew he was fast, and it wasn't something he needed to shout about. Well, except for his race celebrations, which were getting flashier and more dramatic with each victory.

By the time 2016 was winding down, Noah had one last thing to cross off his list: the USA Junior Championships. And wouldn't you know it? He absolutely owned the 100 meters. And if that wasn't enough, he went on to win the gold in the 200 meters and the 4x100-meter relay, a race where four team members each run 100 meters, at the U20 World Championships. It was like he had a golden touch—anything he set foot in turned into a victory.

At this point, Noah had to figure out what came next. College recruiters were circling like seagulls, each one hoping to snatch him up for their team. Noah even considered attending the University of Florida, a powerhouse in track and field. But after some deep thinking and probably a few pep talks from his family, he decided to skip the whole college thing. Why wait to be the best in a few years when you could be the best right now? So, Noah signed a professional deal with Adidas right out of high school, trading his textbooks for sneakers and becoming a pro athlete, meaning he got paid to compete, before most kids had even decided what they wanted to major in. Can you believe that? One minute he's a kid with a nebulizer, and the next he's flying around the world, racking up medals and making deals with a company known for sponsoring some of the greatest athletes in history. And yet, through it all, Noah stayed grounded—well, as grounded as someone who could practically fly across the track could be.

With his track career officially launched, Noah was ready to take on the world—or at least every track he set foot on. The boy who once battled asthma had grown into a sprinter whose feet were practically on fire. The road ahead wasn't always clear, but Noah had one thing on his mind: running so fast that no one could ever catch him.

Once Noah Lyles leaped into the world of professional track, there was no turning back. His shoes were laced, his goals were set, and the world was about to witness the rise of a sprinter who could make history books sweat trying to keep up. Noah had his sights set on greatness—the kind of greatness you read about in comic books or see in the movies. He was running to chase down legends. More specifically, one legend: Usain Bolt. You see, Usain Bolt was like the ultimate superhero in the world of sprinting. The guy was faster than fast. With world records (the fastest times ever officially recorded) in the 100-meter and 200-meter events, Bolt's name was practically written in the sky, and for years, it seemed like no one could catch him. But Noah… Well, he had other plans. It was his goal. Noah once said, "I've always known that I'm the fastest man in the world. Well, in my head, I think I'm going to break it. I'm planning to break it." And let me tell you, when Noah Lyles plans to do something, you better believe he's serious.

After signing his deal with Adidas, Noah was ready to take on the world—literally. And in 2017, the world began to take notice. At the U.S. Indoor Championships, Noah set a new world record in the 300 meters, beating the previous one by just 1/100th of a second, which is an incredibly tiny amount of time. It was as if he wasn't racing against other athletes; he was racing against the clock itself. The time was 31.87 seconds—lightning-fast for an indoor event (which is run inside a building). This victory was like the opening credits to an action movie, except instead of explosions and car chases, you had Noah zooming past everyone in sight.

Fast-forward to 2019, and Noah's career hit warp speed. He competed at the World Championships in Doha, Qatar, one of the biggest events in track and field, only second to the Olympics, where the entire globe had its eyes glued to the track. He was the favorite to win the 200 meters. And guess what? He didn't disappoint. With a time of 19.83 seconds, an incredibly fast time, only a bit slower than Usain Bolt's world record, Noah blazed through the competition and took home his first world title in the 200 meters. If you were paying attention, you'd realize that this was more than just a victory—it was a statement. He was coming for the throne.

But here's the thing about Noah: he was never satisfied. He wanted to do it with flair, with style. Whether he was crossing the finish line with a triumphant roar or pulling off some wild celebration that had the crowd buzzing, Noah was turning sprinting into an event. Fans couldn't get enough of him. He wasn't afraid to be himself—whether that meant rocking crazy hairstyles or rapping in his free time under the name "Nojo18." He was like a real-life superhero, bursting with personality, speed, and a fierce determination to shake up the world of track and field. And that's exactly what he did.

By 2022, Noah was back at it, this time at the World Championships in Eugene, Oregon. Once again, he lined up for the 200 meters, and once again, he flew past everyone like they were standing still. His time: 19.31 seconds. Let that sink in for a sec. He broke Michael Johnson's American record, which had stood untouched for 23 years. It was the third-fastest time ever recorded in the history of the event. And Noah was grinning from ear to ear. The gold medal hung around his neck, but what he really had his eye on was Usain Bolt's 19.19 world record. It was still out there, dangling like a carrot, taunting him.

As if that wasn't enough, in 2023, Noah pulled off a feat that hadn't been seen since the days of Usain Bolt himself. At the World Championships in Budapest, he completed the sprint treble—winning the 100 meters, 200 meters, and the 4x100-meter relay, three gold medals in the main sprinting events. It was the kind of performance that made jaws drop, and suddenly, people weren't just comparing him to Bolt—they were wondering if he might actually surpass him. "I've always known I'm the fastest man in the world," Noah said after the championships. And you know what? He had the gold medals to prove it.

The 100 meters, in particular, was a milestone for Noah. Known primarily for his dominance in the 200 meters, he had always been seen as a 200-meter specialist. But now, by winning the 100 meters as well, Noah was proving that he could do it all. He clocked a blistering 9.83 seconds in the 100 meters, an incredibly fast time, showing the world that he wasn't just about the 200 anymore. This was a new chapter—one where Noah was staking his claim as the world's fastest man, period.

And then, in 2024, the moment arrived that Noah had been waiting for his entire life—the Paris Olympics. After winning bronze in the 200 meters back in Tokyo 2020, Noah knew this was his chance to claim the title of Olympic champion. But it wasn't going to be easy. The competition was fierce, and the pressure? Oh, it was through the roof.

Noah thrived under pressure. The Olympic stadium was packed, the world was watching, and Noah stepped onto the track with one goal in mind: win.

In the 100 meters, the showdown was set. Noah's biggest competition was Jamaica's Kishane Thompson, a sprinter who could practically match Noah stride for stride. The race was so close that when they crossed the finish line, nobody could tell who won. Officials had to consult the high-speed camera (a special camera that can see incredibly fast movements) to figure it out. The crowd held its breath. And then, it was announced: Noah Lyles had won. By just five-thousandths of a second (that's 0.005 seconds—an incredibly tiny margin), he had edged out Thompson to claim the gold medal. Noah tore off his name tag, waving it in triumph as he ran his victory lap, basking in the roar of the crowd. This was Noah's first Olympic gold in the 100 meters, the one event he had missed out on in Tokyo.

Of course, Noah went on to also claim bronze in the 200 meters—never enough for him—an event he had dominated for years. But something was off. Noah wasn't his usual explosive self. Turns out, he had been diagnosed with COVID just two days before the race. Even with the illness weighing him down, Noah still managed to make the podium, finishing in the top three and get a medal. That, my friends, is the definition of determination!

Our running champion had made a promise to himself—to take his sport to new heights, to go beyond the world of track and field like Usain Bolt and the swimmer Michael Phelps before him. He wanted to be a household name. He even organized a red-carpet-style walk-in, like the fancy entrances at big Hollywood events, but for athletes, at the 2023 New York City Grand Prix because, in his own words, "Why aren't there any track and field people in here?" He wanted to inject some glamour into the sport, to make track stars as famous as football players or NBA superstars.

Beyond the track, he's an advocate for mental health, openly sharing his own struggles and the value of therapy in his life. He's been vocal about breaking the stigma (negative attitudes) around mental health in sports, especially for young athletes who, like him, face immense pressure. "I've been in therapy since I was probably 9 years old," Noah said, showing once again that his strength was more importantly in his heart and mind!

And so, as the fastest man in the world stood on the podium at the Paris Olympics, he was thinking about the future—about how to inspire the next generation of sprinters, about how to push his sport into the spotlight, and, yes, about how he was going to chase down Usain Bolt's records. "The sky's the limit," he once said. But for Noah Lyles, maybe even the sky isn't fast enough.

Katie Ledecky

"INSPIRING WOMEN"
... RULING THE DEPTHS OF DISTANCE SWIMMING

If we go back to the early 2000s, in the neighborhoods surrounding Washington, D. C.—where the Potomac River winds through historic landmarks and suburban pools shimmered like tiny oases on hot summer days. Katie Ledecky was just a small, water-loving tadpole in human form. I mean, we're talking about a kid who, by all accounts, was probably more comfortable in the water than most of us are on dry land. Katie was born in 1997, in the bustling, political powerhouse city of Washington, D.C. But her true roots were firmly planted in the suburban tranquility of Bethesda, Maryland, a peaceful area just outside the city. This is where our story kicks off—a story that would eventually lead to the makings of a swimming legend, although back then, it all started with a splash!

Katie was your classic kid-next-door—except with a twist. While other kids her age were busy learning how to ride bikes or organizing lemonade stands, Katie was busy racking up laps (swimming back and forth many times) at the local pool with her swim team, the Palisades Porpoises. But before you get the wrong idea and think she was some sort of mini Aquagirl from the get-go, let's set the record straight: young Katie Ledecky was a "truly mediocre swimmer" when she first started, or so she claimed. Can you believe it? That's like a wizard saying they were really just a so-so wand-waver before hitting Hogwarts.

She first dipped her toes into the swimming world at the ripe old age of six, thanks to the gentle nudging of her mom, Mary Gen, who herself was a collegiate swimmer. Katie's early years in the pool were a mix of typical childhood antics (playful behavior) and surprising dedication. Her parents, both graduates of the well-known and highly respected university, Harvard, noticed Katie's knack for swimming almost immediately. She had this remarkable ability to float and glide through the water like she'd been doing it since birth. It wasn't long before the Ledecky household realized they might have something special on their hands—or rather, in their pool.

Katie's older brother, Michael, was also a swimmer, and the sibling rivalry (competition between brothers and sisters) was real. I mean, you know how it is: brothers and sisters competing over everything, from who gets to control the TV remote to who can swim the fastest lap. But here's where it gets interesting. One fateful summer day, Katie challenged Michael to a 200-meter freestyle race (that's four lengths of an Olympic-sized pool, where swimmers use the front crawl stroke). Now, keep in mind, Michael was not some lazy weekend swimmer. He was a serious, high-achieving teenager with hopes of swimming for an Ivy League team someday, which are teams from prestigious universities like Harvard, Yale, and Princeton. So, he confidently agreed to the race, thinking he'd easily smoke his younger sister, I mean, he thought he'd win easily. Hum, he was actually wrong. Katie not only beat Michael, but she also left him with a mix of pride and annoyance as he tried to figure out how his little sister managed to out-swim him in his primary sport. Let's just say, Michael's goggles didn't survive the defeat—yep, he literally broke them in half!

By the time she was 12, she was already waking up at 4:15 AM for practice, following in her brother's footsteps, but with even more determination. This was a full-blown lifestyle. Katie was putting in the miles—about 40 miles a week in the pool, to be precise. Forty miles. That's like swimming back and forth across a football field more than 700 times every week! Talk about dedication. And remember, this was all before she even hit her teenage years.

Her rise was rapid. By eighth grade (around age 13-14), Katie was already competing against swimmers who were four years older than her, and guess what? She was winning by far. Katie set a national age group record (meaning she swam faster than any other girl her age in the country), breaking one that had stood since the 1970s, a record that lasted for over 30 years. Imagine being that young and already shattering records older than your parents' vinyl collection. It was around this time that her family, her coaches, and probably even her pet goldfish began to realize that Katie was extraordinary. But here's the thing about Katie: Sure, she had some innate ability and natural talent, but she also had this insatiable drive to improve, to work on her craft, and to be the best.

One of her early coaches, Bruce Gemmell, noticed this right away. He would introduce a new technique or a minor tweak to her stroke, and unlike most kids who would practice it a couple of times and then move on, Katie would stick with it. She would work on it obsessively, every single day, until it became second nature, so natural that she didn't have to think about it. It didn't matter if it was a small adjustment to her breathing technique or a new turn style; Katie was like a sponge, soaking up every bit of knowledge and squeezing out every drop of effort.

By the time she was 14, Katie and her coach at the time, Yuri Suguiyama, stumbled upon what can only be described as a "eureka moment", a sudden, brilliant idea. They refined a freestyle technique based on Michael Phelps' "galloping" stroke (Michael Phelps is one of the most famous swimmers ever, and his "galloping" stroke is a unique way of swimming freestyle with a strong, rhythmic motion), and it was as if Katie had unlocked a new level in her swimming game. From that point on, her progression was nothing short of meteoric, incredibly fast. She was starting to dominate not just local competitions but national ones, too.

Her first major splash (pun totally intended) came in 2012 when, as a 15-year-old high school freshman (first year of high school), Katie qualified for the U.S. Olympic Team.

She was the youngest member of the team, and also the most modest and unassuming. At the London Olympics, while all eyes were on the established stars and heavy favorites, this shy teenager with braces and a big smile quietly went about her business. And by "business," I mean she went on to win a gold medal in the 800-meter freestyle (that's 16 lengths of the pool—a long-distance race). No big deal, right? Except it was a huge deal. Katie's time of 8:14.63 was the second-fastest in history at that point (only one person had ever swum faster), and it catapulted her from "promising youngster" to "swimming prodigy" practically overnight. But if you thought Katie would let all the newfound fame and glory get to her head, you'd be wrong. Despite her newfound status as an Olympic champion, she remained the same humble and down to earth, hardworking teenager from Bethesda. She continued to train diligently, pushing herself to new limits and refining her craft with the same relentless focus she'd always had. For Katie, it was never about the medals or the accolades. It was about the love of the sport, the joy of competition, and the satisfaction of knowing she was doing her best.

There you have it—the early years of Katie Ledecky, from backyard swim meets to Olympic glory. And believe me, this is just the beginning. Katie's story is one of incredible talent, hard work, and a little bit of sibling rivalry thrown in for good measure.

So, Katie had officially burst onto the world stage at just 15 years old, grabbing a gold medal at the 2012 London Olympics like it was no big deal. But this was only the beginning. Winning that gold didn't mean she could just kick back with a smoothie and some Netflix. This was where the real work began, and Katie, well, she was all in.

After London, Katie's life went from "school-kid-who's-good-at-swimming" to "prodigy-who-needs-to-swim-all-the-time." If swimming was a video game, Katie was unlocking all the levels. She started training with the legendary coach Bruce Gemmell, and together they formed a duo that would become the stuff of legend. Bruce, who had seen his fair share of talented swimmers, knew that Katie was different. She had the kind of work ethic that could make even the laziest person in the world want to get off the couch.

Her training routine was intense. Like, really intense. I mean, her daily schedule could make even the busiest bee feel lazy. A typical day in the life of Katie Ledecky around this time was a testament to her dedication. She was up before the sun—4:05 AM, to be exact. And let's be real, most of us aren't even dreaming at that hour, let alone swimming laps. By 5 AM, Katie was already in the pool, churning out 6,000 to 6,500 yards (that's about 3.5 to 3.7 miles) before most people had their first cup of coffee. It's no wonder she's a world champion. After that grueling session, it was time for a hearty breakfast—think omelets or bagels with cream cheese, all washed down with her favorite, chocolate milk. Because, apparently, chocolate milk is the breakfast of champions.

After her morning session and a nap (yep, she squeezed those in too), she'd hit the gym for dryland training. We're talking strength training, core workouts, and all those exercises that make the rest of us groan just thinking about them. Then, it was back to the pool for another session in the afternoon. More laps, more drills, more training. If you think about it, she was practically living in the water. At the end of the day, after dinner and some downtime, she'd hit the hay by 9:15 PM, ready to do it all over again the next day.

Despite all that, her life wasn't all about grueling workouts and early mornings. She made sure to keep things balanced. She's a huge fan of Scrabble and chess—basically, anything that would keep her mind sharp while her body was in training mode. She even played the piano when she had the time. And let's not forget that she's a die-hard New York Islanders fan, thanks in part to her uncle, Jon Ledecky, being a co-owner of the team (the New York Islanders are a professional ice hockey team).

And yes, the road to greatness isn't always smooth. Katie, just like everybody else, faced her fair share of challenges. There was that time in 2019 when she was hit with a stomach virus and couldn't compete in the 200m freestyle at the World Championships in Gwangju (a major international swimming competition). And let's not forget the madness of the COVID-19 pandemic. When the world went into lockdown, pools were closed, competitions were canceled, and athletes everywhere had to adapt. For Katie, this meant training in a backyard pool offered by a generous local family when her usual training spot at Stanford University was shut down (Stanford is a university in California where she was studying and training). Talk about making the best of a bad situation. She even had a cheering squad in the form of the family's grandchildren, who would root for her and her teammate Simone Manuel as they practiced in those makeshift lanes.

Adapting to these challenges wasn't easy, but it was necessary for her; it was a testament to Katie's character. She didn't complain. Instead, she saw it as an opportunity to grow.

She kept her focus, continued her training, and even managed to graduate with a degree in psychology from Stanford University during this time (so she was also working hard on her education). It's like she was living proof of that old saying, "When life gives you lemons, make lemonade." Except, in her case, she was making world-class swimming times and earning a college degree at the same time.

By the time the Tokyo Olympics rolled around in 2021 (delayed a year because of the pandemic), Katie was more than ready to prove herself once again. And prove herself she did. She won gold in both the 800m and 1500m freestyle, making her the first woman ever to win the 1500m event at the Olympics (this was the first time women were allowed to compete in this event at the Olympics). She also picked up silver medals in the 400m freestyle and the 4x200m freestyle relay (a team event where four swimmers each swim 200 meters). It was another incredible performance that solidified her status as one of the greatest swimmers of all time.

After Tokyo, Katie made a big decision to shake up her training routine. She moved from California to Gainesville, Florida, to train under coach Anthony Nesty at the University of Florida. This was a big move, both literally and figuratively. It meant a new environment, new training partners—including Olympic gold medalists like Caeleb Dressel and Bobby Finke—and new challenges. But if there's one thing we know about Katie by now, it's that she thrives on challenges. Her training routine became even more rigorous, if you can believe it, with 10 swim practices and five gym sessions every week.

And it was in this new chapter of her life that Katie continued to develop and refine her skills. She worked tirelessly on her technique, adjusting her stroke, refining her kick, and even recalibrating her rotation. Her coach Anthony Nesty pushed her to become more athletic, and Katie responded as she always does—with hard work and determination.

But what really set Katie apart was her mindset. Yes! Katie had this incredible ability to focus on the process rather than the outcome. Sure, winning medals and breaking records were nice, but for her, it was all about the journey. It was about getting better every day, pushing herself to new limits, and enjoying every moment in the water. She loved the grind, the daily routine of training, the feeling of pushing herself to be the best she could be.

Her discipline and consistency inspired those around her. Teammates, rivals, and even fans all saw in her a dedication that was truly remarkable. She was more than just an athlete; she was a role model, a person who showed that with hard work, perseverance, and a love for what you do, anything is possible. She even earned the nickname "The First Lady of Freestyle," a title that perfectly encapsulated her dominance in the sport.

As Katie continued to push herself, she also kept an eye on the future. She was thinking ahead to the Paris 2024 Olympics. For Katie, it wasn't about chasing records or medals. It was about continuing to do what she loved, representing her country, and inspiring the next generation of swimmers. Katie Ledecky's journey from that backyard pool to the Olympic podium is a story of incredible talent, yes, but also of unparalleled dedication and an unyielding love for the sport.

Katie Ledecky is a force of nature, and, as of the Paris 2024 Olympics, officially the greatest female swimmer of all time. You might be thinking, "Wait, didn't we already know this?" And you wouldn't be wrong! But at Paris, she decided to make it even more official by doing what Katie does best: breaking records and taking names. So let's talk Paris.

By the time she stepped up to the starting blocks at the 2024 Olympics, Katie was already considered the "GOAT" (Greatest of All Time) by many. Yet, she wasn't there to rest on her laurels. She was there to swim, to compete, and to add more gold to her already dazzling collection. And yes, did she deliver! Katie snagged four medals, including two golds, adding up to a total of nine Olympic gold medals. This achievement tied her with the legendary Larisa Latynina, a fantastic gymnast from the Soviet Union, for the most Olympic gold medals ever won by a female athlete in any sport.

Her first gold in Paris came in the 1500m freestyle, where she broke her own Olympic record, showing everyone once again why she's called the "First Lady of Freestyle". In a race that seemed more like a showcase of her utter dominance, she literally wiped out the competition, finishing more than ten seconds ahead of the next swimmer (which is a huge margin in swimming). This victory marked her fourth consecutive gold medal in this event—a feat so rare that it's almost mythical in the world of sports. And she wasn't done yet. She followed up with another spectacular win in the 800m freestyle, securing her place in history with her fourth straight Olympic gold in that event as well. This achievement put her on a very short list of athletes who have four-peated in an individual Olympic event—a list that includes legends like Michael Phelps.

And as if that wasn't enough, Katie's silver medal performance in the 4x200m freestyle relay helped her become the most decorated female swimmer ever in terms of total Olympic medals. By the end of Paris, she had an astounding 14 Olympic medals—second only to Michael Phelps in swimming history (Michael Phelps has 28 Olympic medals). Legendary!

But let's not get too caught up in the medals, because for Katie, it's always been about more than this. Her love for the sport, her discipline, and her relentless drive to improve are what really set her apart. Even after such a historic performance in Paris, when asked about her future, Katie said she was already thinking about getting back in the water. "I probably enjoy the training more than the racing," she admitted. It's that kind of mindset—always looking to improve, always focused on the process—that has defined her career and inspired so many.

And speaking of being an inspiration, Katie's impact goes way beyond just swimming. She's become someone to look up to for anyone trying their best, no matter what they're doing. Her dedication to her craft, her humility despite her success, and her commitment to representing her country with pride have made her a beloved figure worldwide. At Paris, her presence was magnetic—athletes from all sports and countries lined up to meet her, including tennis star Coco Gauff, who initially found Katie's intense focus a bit intimidating until she realized how down-to-earth and approachable she really was.

Katie's kindness and sportsmanship are as renowned as her swimming. After winning her ninth gold medal in Paris, she was seen embracing her competitors, offering encouragement and sharing the podium with teammates. For Katie, it's always been about more than swimming; it's about the relationships, the camaraderie, and the joy of competing at the highest level.

This brings us to her future. Katie is not done yet—not by a long shot. She's already set her sights on the Los Angeles 2028 Olympics, her fifth Games. In her typical modest fashion, she says she's taking things year by year, but it's clear that the fire still burns brightly. She's excited about the prospect of competing on home soil and continuing to inspire the next generation of swimmers. And while the competitive fire is still there, Katie has also been thinking about life beyond the pool. She's expressed interest in mentoring younger athletes and using her platform to promote causes she cares about. In 2024, she released her memoir, "Just Add Water," where she shared her journey and the lessons she's learned along the way. She's been a flagbearer for the Olympic Games Closing Ceremony and was awarded the Presidential Medal of Freedom, which is the the highest civilian award in the United States, underscoring her impact as an athlete, a leader and a role model.

In every sense of the word, Katie Ledecky has locked up her status as the GOAT—Greatest of All Time. For what she's accomplished in the pool, and for how she's carried herself throughout her career. She's shown that greatness is of course about winning, but not only; it's about how you win, how you inspire others, and how you leave a legacy that goes beyond the numbers and the records. So yeah... whether she's breaking records in the pool, mentoring the next wave of swimmers, or using her platform to make a difference in the world, one thing is for sure: Katie Ledecky will continue to be a force for good, a beacon of excellence, and a true legend in every sense of the word!

Steph Curry

"One Three at a Time" ... Dominating Basketball from Deep

Every extraordinary journey begins somewhere, often in ways no one could predict. For Steph Curry, one of basketball's most electrifying stars, that journey started quietly—far from the bright lights of the NBA, our little champ wasn't *always* that guy swishing threes from the half-court like it's no big deal. Once upon a time, little Steph was a pretty regular kid, well, regular if "regular" means having NBA superstar Dell Curry as a dad and a professional volleyball player for a mom. Yeah, no pressure or anything... Steph was born on March 14, 1988, in the exact same hospital where *another* NBA legend was born: LeBron James. Yeah, let that idea simmer in your mind for a bit. Akron, Ohio must've been handing out future NBA GOATs like they were free samples at Costco. But anyway, right after making his grand entrance into the world, Steph, the oldest of three siblings, packed up his baby blankets and settled in North Carolina. This is where the real fun began.

Now, many might assume that Dell Curry, NBA sharpshooter, had baby Steph working on his dribbling skills from day one, but that's not exactly how things unfolded. Dell and Sonya Curry were a *chill* set of parents, letting their kids figure out their own thing. They weren't out there like, "You must shoot 1,000 free throws before bedtime or no dinner!" Nah, Steph, his younger brother Seth (yes, another future NBA player), and their sister Sydel (who's into volleyball, naturally) were all banned from playing competitive sports until middle school. That's right, the future face of basketball couldn't even join a proper team until he was about 11 years old. Can you imagine telling today's Tiger Moms that Steph Curry didn't have a personal trainer in the third grade? Chaos.

But life in the Curry household was more than just *athletic genes waiting to explode*. The family had a massive 16-acre property in Charlotte, North Carolina. Yup, 16 whole acres of pure childhood paradise. It's like living in a park, where the swing set might just be bigger than most people's backyards. Picture little Steph and Seth running around that huge estate with wild ideas, probably trying to invent new sports that involved both basketballs *and* volleyballs, while Sydel spiked anything that flew past her. If you're imagining the Curry kids with more energy than their parents knew how to handle, you're probably spot-on. But for Steph, his dad's job had one major perk that most kids would trade their entire collection of action figures for: unlimited access to NBA games. Being Dell Curry's kid came with VIP access to the *Charlotte Hornets* games, which meant that Steph and Seth were basically living the dream of every basketball-obsessed kid. Imagine being able to chill courtside at your dad's games, casually chatting with NBA stars like it's no big deal. Yeah, casual for the Curry brothers, *life-shattering* for the rest of us.

In fact, one of Steph's earliest memories—brace yourself for a mega throwback—is from when he was *four years old* at the NBA All-Star Weekend. Little toddler Steph, was spending time out on his dad's lap, with legit NBA legends Mitch Richmond and Don Nelson kicking it in the background. You can practically see Steph's wide eyes soaking it all in, probably plotting his future domination even at that age. I mean, when your first memory is at an *All-Star Weekend*, you're bound to do some damage later, right?

But hold up, it wasn't all slam dunks and NBA-level access for young Steph. For a lot of his childhood, he had one major problem: he was short. And skinny. We're talking, "Maybe this kid should've stuck to math camp" levels of small compared to his basketball peers. It didn't help that coaches would take one look at him and think, "Eh, maybe next time, kid." At the time, Steph was what some might call… "fun-sized," which didn't exactly scream "future greatest shooter of all time." But if we've learned anything from every feel-good sports movie ever, it's that you *never* count out the undersized kid with insane basketball IQ. And that was Steph—he might not have had the muscle, but his skills and smarts were already top-tier, even as a kid who could barely look over the counter at McDonald's.

While basketball was obviously destined to be *the thing* for Steph, he wasn't a one-sport wonder. He dabbled in a bit of everything—because why not?—and at age 10, golf suddenly became his side quest. And it wasn't one of those "Oh, I'll try this for five minutes and then move on" hobbies either. No, even as an adult, Steph's still all about the golf life, showing up in celebrity tournaments and sinking birdies like it's part of his NBA training regime. I mean, if you can shoot threes under pressure, you can probably sink a hole-in-one while chatting it up with pros like Andre Iguodala. (Fun fact: Steph *legit* calls golf his therapy. Meanwhile, I eat Oreos when I'm stressed. To each their own, I guess.) … Of course, basketball and golf weren't enough for young Steph. He also tried his hand at baseball, stepping up to the plate with the same intensity he'd later bring to the court. Steph's dad, Dell, was a pitcher, but Steph? He preferred hitting. And, surprise surprise, he wasn't too shabby at it, leading his baseball team to a state championship. But, being the multi-talented legend that he is, Steph eventually had to let baseball go to focus on basketball. Which, honestly, worked out fine for everyone, especially for the NBA.

Before we move on to the next part of Steph's life, we've got to talk about *that one time* the Curry family packed up and moved to *Toronto* because Dell had been traded to the Raptors. That meant Steph, still a kid, was adjusting to a whole new city, a whole new basketball vibe, and yes, he even had to learn how to say "eh" and "aboot." But Toronto wasn't just a random pit stop on his way to greatness—it's where Steph's basketball legend began to truly form. He joined the boys' basketball team at Queensway Christian College, a tiny school with all of 200 students. With Steph dropping 40-50 points per game, it probably felt like the other teams were just there to give him practice. And they went undefeated, and that was all Steph—making magic with his undersized frame and oversized skills... Okay, so we're at the point where young Steph is starting to realize that his path might just be paved with three-pointers, buzzer-beaters, and maybe a few NBA championships. But for now, we'll leave him as the scrawny kid lighting it up in Toronto, shooting threes long before it was cool, and setting the stage for what would become a mind-blowing career.

Alright, so young Steph Curry is making waves in Toronto, dropping 50 points like it's some casual Sunday afternoon hobby. But let's fast-forward a little because the Curry family didn't stay in the land of maple syrup forever. By the time Steph hit high school, they had moved back to Charlotte, North Carolina. And while Toronto gave us the glimpse of Curry magic, it was in Charlotte where things started to get serious. Steph enrolled in *Charlotte Christian School*, where he probably didn't have to explain who his dad was because, duh, Dell Curry was basically a legend by now. But Steph wasn't riding on his dad's coattails. He was out there grinding, putting in the hours, and getting ready to *prove* that just because his last name was Curry didn't mean he was about to get a free pass. Nah, this dude worked. Hard. And it paid off—big time. During his high school career, he led the Charlotte Christian team to *three* conference titles and three state playoffs. Not bad for a kid who still wasn't getting much attention from scouts because of—you guessed it—his size.

It's wild to think about now, but back then, the biggest problem wasn't Steph's skills or his basketball IQ (both of which were off the charts). It was his *height*. Coaches would take one look at him, all skinny and short, and immediately move on. Like, can you imagine someone being like, "Hmm, I don't think Steph Curry has what it takes?" Blasphemy. The guy was out there torching teams, but since he hadn't hit that late growth spurt yet, people kept sleeping on him. This is your regular reminder that *never* judging a book by its cover should be the rule, not the exception.

Now, here's the kicker: despite *dominating* high school hoops and practically owning the three-point line, Steph wasn't exactly swamped with scholarship offers. In fact, he wasn't even ranked in the *Rivals Top 150*. He was out there waiting for someone to notice that maybe—just maybe—this undersized dude could actually be kind of good at basketball. And, of course, his dream school was Virginia Tech, where his parents met, fell in love, and probably imagined raising a basketball prodigy. But here's where the universe throws in a curveball: Virginia Tech didn't exactly roll out the red carpet for Steph. They offered him a *walk-on* spot, which, let's be real, is basically like saying, "Yeah, sure, you can *technically* play for us, but don't expect us to be too excited about it." ... Steph, though? He wasn't having any of that walk-on nonsense. He decided to take his talents to *Davidson College*, a small school that had been keeping an eye on him since the 10th grade. And here's where things get good. Steph goes to Davidson, a school not known for being a basketball winning machine, and from the *second* he steps on the court, the kid starts breaking records like it's his side hustle. In his freshman year, he became the second-highest scorer in the entire country. Yup, the only person who scored more points than him that year was none other than Kevin Durant. You know, just a future Hall of Famer, no big deal. But Steph wasn't just piling up points for fun. He was leading his team to wins. Like, *a lot* of wins. His three-point shot was already terrifying defenders, and he was only a *freshman*. By the end of that first season, he'd broken the NCAA freshman record for most three-pointers in a season with a ridiculous 122 bombs from downtown. He wasn't even warming up yet.

Sophomore year rolled around, and Steph had grown into his 6'3" frame. This is where Davidson became *the* Cinderella story of the NCAA Tournament. You know how every year there's that one team that nobody sees coming, and suddenly they're knocking off the big boys? That was Davidson, with Steph Curry leading the charge like some kind of three-point-draining wizard. The Wildcats went on a rampage through the NCAA Tournament, and Steph was out there torching *everyone*. Gonzaga? See ya. Georgetown? Bye-bye. Wisconsin? Nah, man. All these higher-seeded teams were no match for Davidson's *secret weapon*. They made it all the way to the *Elite 8*, which is a big deal for a small school that probably had *never* seen this kind of success before. Here's the crazy part: during this run, Steph was *literally* changing the game. Like, up until this point, sure, people shot threes, but not like *this*. Steph was pulling up from distances that most coaches would scream at you for even thinking about. But for him? It was all net, all day. At one point, Steph even set the NCAA record for most three-pointers in a single season with 159. For context, some teams don't even shoot that many threes in a season. Steph was out there *making* that many, no biggie.

Naturally, after that wild tournament run, people started talking about whether Curry should *make the jump* to the NBA right away. You know, go pro, start cashing those checks. And honestly, no one would've blamed him. His stock was rising faster than the price of concert tickets when Beyoncé's in town. But Steph was different. He wasn't *just* about the fame or the money. He wanted to be *better*. So, what did he do? He went back to Davidson for his junior season to work on his skills as a point guard. Because, yeah, being the best shooter anyone's ever seen wasn't enough—he wanted to get even *better* at handling the ball and running plays. Talk about commitment.

In his junior year, Steph was still lighting up the scoreboard like it was his personal hobby. In one game, he dropped a career-high *44 points*. Then, in another, he dished out 13 assists, like "Oh, you want some points? Here, take them, I've got plenty to spare." But of course, basketball isn't *always* sunshine and rainbows, even when you're Steph Curry. He also had one brutal game where he didn't score a single point—0 for 3 from the field. Yup, zero points. To be fair, the guy was double-teamed for the entire game, so, like, can we *really* blame him? But that little blip didn't slow him down. By the end of his junior year, Steph was averaging an *insane* 28.6 points per game, with 5.6 assists and 2.5 steals to go along with it. Oh, and he casually led the nation in scoring. No big deal. That's just what you do when you're Steph Curry, apparently. He was also named to the All-American first team, because, let's be real, at this point, was there anyone more deserving?

Despite his individual success, Davidson's NCAA Tournament run didn't quite match the magic of the previous year. But by then, it didn't matter—Steph had done more than enough to prove that he was NBA-ready. Everyone and their grandma knew that it was time for Steph to go pro. He'd spent three years dominating the college scene, transforming a little-known school into a nationally recognized basketball force. Now, all that was left was to see where his professional journey would take him. So, you got it, there was Steph Curry, the college phenom, the kid who turned doubters into believers, and turned a small school into a basketball powerhouse—all with the flick of his wrist from beyond the arc.

Alright, so we've left college Steph on the edge of greatness, dropping bombs from the three-point line and making college defenses look like they were guarding him with *pool noodles*. Now, it's 2009, and the NBA is calling—loudly. Enter the *NBA Draft*, where a baby-faced Curry, fresh off wrecking college defenses, gets picked seventh overall by the *Golden State Warriors*. Yep, seventh. Some teams thought there were six other players better than Steph Curry. Fast forward a few years, and those GMs are probably still lying awake at night wondering how they let the greatest shooter in history *slip* past them. Oops. Steph hit the league like a kid at Disneyland for the first time, wide-eyed but ready to *take over*. In his rookie year, he played in 80 games, putting up some *wild* stats: 17.5 points, 4.5 rebounds, 1.9 steals, and 5.9 assists per game. The dude was already filling up the stat sheet like he had been here before, casually dishing dimes and sinking shots like he'd been *born* on the hardwood. Oh wait, technically, he was—remember Akron, Ohio, same hospital as LeBron? Yeah. Rookie Steph was putting everyone on notice, though he ended up as the *runner-up* for Rookie of the Year, losing to Tyreke Evans. That's cool, though—Steph's real flex wasn't going to be *awards*; it was going to be *history*.

But here's where we take a bit of a detour because the basketball gods didn't make Steph Curry's path to NBA superstardom as smooth as his jumper. No, they threw some *ankle problems* his way, just to see if he was really about that life. And these weren't your regular, run-of-the-mill ankle sprains. We're talking *major* injuries that sidelined him for chunks of the 2011-12 season. In fact, he only played in *26 games* that year, and a lot of people were starting to wonder if Curry's ankles were made of glass. The Warriors, though, showed *major* faith and signed him to a four-year, $44 million contract extension. And, let's be real, at that point, people were calling it a risky bet, like putting your life savings on a horse named "Limping Lightning." But as we now know, Golden State's gamble paid off *huge*. Once his ankles were fixed up, Steph came back stronger than ever. And in the 2012-13 season, something *magical* happened: Steph Curry turned into the *three-point god* we all know today. He casually broke the NBA's single-season three-point record by hitting *272 threes*—a number that had only been a dream before Steph came along and redefined what "range" even meant. And that was *just the beginning*.

Then, in 2014, the Warriors made a *key move*: hiring *Steve Kerr* as their head coach. Kerr, a sharpshooter himself, looked at Steph and basically said, "Shoot more, man. Let it fly." And boy, did Curry take that advice to heart. With the green light from Kerr, Steph went from shooting 39.1% of his shots from deep to an astronomical 56.4%. If the NBA was the Wild West, Steph was out there gunning from way past the saloon, launching threes that looked insane—except they were *all* going in. The result? The Warriors morphed into a *superteam*. In 2015, they won their first NBA championship in 40 years, defeating LeBron James and the Cleveland Cavaliers in the finals. Oh, and Steph? He picked up his first *MVP* award, because why not? But the *real* showstopper came in 2016, when Curry absolutely *exploded*. Not only did he lead the league in scoring with *30.1 points per game*, but he also became the first player to make over *400* three-pointers in a single season. That's not just changing the game; that's completely breaking the game and rewriting the rules with a flick of the wrist. The *insane* part? Steph was *so* dominant that season, he became the first-ever NBA player to be named *MVP by unanimous vote*. You read that right: *every* single vote went to Steph. I mean, at this point, the three-point line might as well have been renamed "Steph's Office" because that's where he did *all* his business. But—oh yeah, there's always a "but"—even after leading the Warriors to a *73-9* regular season record (yep, the best ever), they ended up losing to the Cavs in the finals after blowing a *3-1* lead. Ouch. LeBron came back with *that* block, Kyrie hit *that* shot, and Steph's magical season ended with a sting. So what do you do when you have the greatest regular season ever but fall short in the finals? You bounce back—*hard*. In 2017, the Warriors added *Kevin Durant* to their already stacked roster, and they cruised to back-to-back championships in 2017 and 2018. Steph might have shared the spotlight with KD, but make no mistake—he was still out there raining threes, making defenders look like they were trying to guard a ghost. The Warriors were *untouchable*, and Steph's *legacy* as one of the greatest shooters (if not *the* greatest) in NBA history was cemented.

But even superheroes get hit with kryptonite, and for Steph, it came in the form of injuries. In the 2019-2020 season, Curry broke his hand, limiting him to just five games. The Warriors, without their sharpshooting leader, tumbled to the bottom of the standings, and the world got a rare glimpse of a *Curry-less* Warriors squad. The bright side? Steph came back the next season, better than ever, resetting records like it was his day job. He ended up breaking the record for *most threes in a month* with *96* in April 2021 and claimed his second *NBA scoring title* that season.

Now, at this point, Steph had basically rewritten the entire *three-point* chapter of the basketball rulebook. In December 2021, he surpassed Ray Allen to become the *all-time leader* in three-pointers made. Allen's 2,973 threes were legendary, but Steph breezed past that, like, "Thanks for holding my spot, but I've got this now." By the end of the 2022-23 season, Steph had racked up *3,390 regular-season threes*, with *another 690* in the playoffs, pushing his total past *4,000*. That's right—four *thousand* threes. And this man isn't done yet.

Let's jump to *Paris 2024*, where Steph's basketball greatness reached new heights. After all those years, there was one thing missing from Curry's already stacked trophy case—an *Olympic gold medal*. Yeah, *how* is it possible that one of the greatest players of all time hadn't yet played in the Olympics? Well, better late than never. Curry made his *Olympic debut* in Paris at the age of 36, teaming up with guys like Kevin Durant, Devin Booker, and LeBron James. And if you thought Curry was going to treat the Olympics like a vacation, think again.

In the final against France, with the whole world watching, Steph did what Steph *does*. He drained *four* of his *eight* three-pointers in the last few minutes of the game, completely shutting down any hopes of a French comeback. France had Victor Wembanyama, the 7-foot-5 basketball alien who was supposed to be the future of basketball, but guess what? Steph said, "Hold my Gatorade" and put on a show. With 24 points overall, Steph led Team USA to a *98-87* win, securing their fifth straight gold medal. Classic Curry—he saved his best for the biggest stage.

After the game, Curry's reaction was as cool as you'd expect: "I was just trying to settle us down," he said, with that iconic, boyish grin. "At that point, your mind goes blank. You don't really care about the setting or the scenario or anything. It's just a shot." I mean, it's a *bit* more than just a shot when you're closing out the *Olympic finals*, but this is Steph Curry we're talking about—the guy makes the impossible look casual.

With that gold medal in hand, Curry's resume became even more untouchable. Four NBA championships, two MVPs (one *unanimous*), the all-time three-point leader, and now an *Olympic champion*. The dude is basically a walking cheat code for basketball. And what's next for Steph? More threes, probably. The way things are going, he'll likely be sinking shots from the *parking lot* well into his 40s. Maybe he'll even introduce a *half-court line* just to keep things interesting. Because if there's one thing we know for sure about Steph Curry, it's that he's far from done redefining the game. Every time you think you've seen his best, he steps up and *raises the bar*. You can almost hear the defenders across the league collectively groaning: "Here we go again..."

Lindsey Horan

"From Golden to Gold" ... Leading Soccer with Grit and Glory

Some teenagers dream of making it big one day, while others quietly take the first bold steps toward greatness without waiting for permission. Lindsey Horan was one of the latter. Amid the buzz of homework, after-school activities, and weekend adventures, Lindsey was lacing up her boots and setting sights on a path that no other American girl had dared to walk before her. Born on May 26, 1994, in Golden, Colorado, this Gemini—yeah, you heard that right, Geminis tend to get things done—had soccer running through her veins from a young age. But what truly set her apart? It wasn't just her raw talent. It was her *fire*. The type of drive that would make you rethink your Netflix binge and wonder if you should, like, *get up and do something epic.*

So here's the thing: Lindsey's soccer journey didn't follow the traditional path. Normally, an American soccer player, especially a girl, would go through the whole process of playing high school soccer, graduating, and then maybe earning a college scholarship. But not Lindsey. High school soccer? Pfft, that wasn't even on her radar. No, she skipped all that. Lindsey, from the start, had her eye on bigger things. She was 15 years old, scoring goals like nobody's business, and already playing for the U.S. U-17 Women's National Team. To put that into perspective, while most of us were figuring out high school lockers, she was putting on her cleats to represent her country. Instead of playing for Golden High School like any regular kid, Lindsey committed her energy to the Colorado Rush Development Academy, training with U-15 and U-16 boys. Yeah, boys. But even that wasn't challenging enough for her, so she went on to train with the U-17 *Nike Boys* team. That's when you know you're serious—when you're pushing yourself to compete with the best of the best, regardless of the fact that you're not even in the same league (literally). Let's be real, playing alongside boys at that age was no easy feat, but she crushed it. Lindsey, even as a teenager, had this fierce, undeniable drive that made her stand out on any field she stepped onto.

By the time 2012 rolled around, Lindsey had a major decision to make. She was already being touted as the number-one-ranked college prospect by ESPN, with a shiny full-ride scholarship to the University of North Carolina waiting for her. To the average soccer player, that's like being handed a golden ticket. North Carolina is *the* dream school for young soccer stars. But of course, Lindsey wasn't average, was she? Instead of following the beaten path, she did something absolutely groundbreaking. She waved goodbye to her college dreams and the soccer scholarship that so many others would have grabbed onto in a heartbeat. At just 18, Lindsey signed a professional contract with Paris Saint-Germain. Let that sink in for a second. Straight out of high school, this girl made the leap—no, more like a catapult—into professional soccer in Europe, a continent known for its deep soccer culture. PSG wasn't just any random club. We're talking about one of the biggest, most historic soccer clubs on the planet. And she was the first American woman to make such a bold move, bypassing college to go pro overseas. Yeah, Lindsey was making history before she could even legally rent a car in the U.S.

Her parents, Mark and Linda Horan, had raised a determined, gritty kid. They weren't strangers to supporting their daughter's ambitious soccer dreams. But even they must've been floored by Lindsey's decision. Leaving home at such a young age, flying across the world to a country where she didn't even speak the language? It wasn't some casual vacation. It was a massive, life-altering choice. It was a unique moment, 18-year-old Lindsey, standing there in Paris, signing her name on a contract worth six figures with a club as massive as PSG. The weight of the decision must've been intense, right? But here's the thing—she didn't even know French. Can you picture stepping into an environment where you can't understand the coaches, your teammates, or anyone else around you? Lesser mortals would have packed their bags and headed home after the first week of not being able to order a sandwich. But not Lindsey. She learned French. By herself. That's some next-level determination.

Paris was, as they say, a "learning experience" for Lindsey. She arrived with high hopes, eager to prove herself, and of course, she did—46 goals in 58 appearances isn't something you can ignore. But the challenges? Yeah, they were real. PSG, for all its glamour, had some darker undertones. There was pressure to fit a mold—*their* mold. Lindsey faced intense body shaming from the club's staff, criticism that was less about her performance and more about appearances. They wanted her to be thinner, to look a certain way, regardless of the fact that she was excelling on the pitch... For Lindsey, it got to a point where she started to lose herself. Her weight was criticized so frequently that she drastically cut down on food to unhealthy levels. Imagine feeling like you've got zero energy because you're trying to meet unrealistic, superficial standards while still being expected to perform at the highest level. An assistant coach even had the audacity to slap a snack out of her hand. Yeah, you heard that right. They were fining players for eating dessert. It wasn't about fitness anymore; it was about image, and it pushed Lindsey to a dark place, one where she started questioning everything—including her love for the game.

But despite all that, Lindsey didn't quit. She could have walked away from soccer right then and there. But she didn't. She gritted her teeth and got through it. The experience hardened her, not in a bad way, but in a way that gave her an unshakable resolve. She went on to thrive in PSG, not because of the environment but in spite of it. Lindsey scored goals, made a name for herself, and paved the way for other American players to take that risk of going pro straight out of high school... Even so, her time at PSG was bittersweet, and by the end of 2015, she was ready to head back home. Her contract with PSG was terminated on January 4, 2016, and though she loved the soccer culture in Europe, there was something about returning to the States that felt right. But before she left, she made sure to leave her mark on the French league—one final match, one final goal, a 5–0 victory over FCF Juvisy. Classic Lindsey, going out with a bang. Next chapter? Portland Thorns. But we'll get to that.

Returning to the States after those four intense years at PSG, Lindsey Horan wasn't the same wide-eyed teenager she had been when she first left for Europe. She was stronger. She had scars, both physical and emotional, from the battles she faced on and off the pitch. But she was ready to turn a new page, to focus on building a legacy back home, and honestly? Portland Thorns FC was the perfect place to do that. By January 2016, Lindsey had officially signed with the Portland Thorns, one of the powerhouse clubs in the National Women's Soccer League (NWSL). From the moment she set foot in the Rose City, she wasn't there to play around. She was there to win, to lead, and to remind everyone exactly who Lindsey Horan was—a player shaped by European grit but with that raw American edge. But before we dive into her Portland years, let's take a second to appreciate how wild this was: Horan had gone from high schooler in Colorado to playing in Paris for four years, and now she was back on home soil, not as a newbie, but as a seasoned pro. That's not your average 21-year-old's life story, is it?

Now, one of the coolest things about Lindsey's transition to Portland was her switch in roles. At PSG, she was a forward, and we know she crushed it there with her insane goal count. But for the Thorns? She shifted into a central midfield position. I know, I know—why mess with success, right? But here's where you see Horan's soccer IQ on full display. This was more than a position change. It was a strategic move that showcased her versatility. Playing in midfield allowed Lindsey to use her vision, her leadership, and her sheer ability to dominate the game, not just with goals but with controlling the flow of the match. She wasn't just there to score anymore—she was there to run the show. It didn't take long for her to make an impact. In fact, by the end of her very first season with the Thorns, she had already helped the team lift the NWSL Shield for having the best regular season record in the league. And yeah, she wasn't just along for the ride—Lindsey was one of the key players making things happen. But 2017? Oh man, that's when Lindsey truly cemented her legacy in Portland.

The Thorns had made it to the NWSL Championship final, and it was no walk in the park. They were up against the North Carolina Courage, one of the most intense, high-energy teams in the league. It was one of those games where every touch of the ball, every pass, every tackle mattered. And guess who came through with the clutch moment? Yep, Lindsey Horan. She scored the only goal in the match, sealing the 1-0 victory for Portland and handing them the championship. One goal, one defining moment, and Lindsey was crowned the game's MVP. But let's be honest, it wasn't just the goal—it was the way she commanded the field. That's what made her invaluable. Portland fans? Yeah, they were officially in love with her by that point.

Off the field, she was growing into one of the most respected voices in women's soccer. The NWSL had its fair share of star players, but Lindsey was stepping into a different kind of spotlight. She was a leader. That leadership quality started to show not just in her performances but in the way she connected with her teammates. Becky Sauerbrunn, a veteran in her own right, would later talk about how much she admired Horan's ability to bridge the gap between the veterans and the younger players. Lindsey had this unique ability to relate to everyone, whether it was a fresh-faced rookie like Mallory Swanson (formerly Pugh) or a seasoned pro like Megan Rapinoe. That's the kind of quality that can't be taught. In fact, this leadership was starting to get recognized on a national level. By 2021, Lindsey was named co-captain of the U.S. Women's National Team (USWNT) alongside the iconic Alex Morgan. Let's pause here for a sec. The USWNT has seen some of the most legendary captains in soccer history—Abby Wambach, Christie Rampone, Carla Overbeck—so to be handed that responsibility at just 27? Yeah, it's a big deal. And she wasn't just stepping into a role of "co-captain" in name. She was becoming the heartbeat of the team, leading them into battle with the same determination she had carried through PSG and Portland. It wasn't always easy though. With leadership comes pressure, and for someone like Horan, who had grown up preferring to let her play do the talking, being vocal in this role was an adjustment. But it was one she embraced fully. She had a mission now: to carry the torch for the USWNT and to make sure the next generation of players had someone to look up to.

Oh, and let's not forget 2018—a huge year for Lindsey. That season, she was named NWSL MVP. I mean, how could she not be? She was an absolute machine that year, scoring goals, breaking up plays, and dictating the pace of every game like she had a remote control to the entire field. She was named Player of the Month in July 2018, after leading the Thorns to a perfect 3-0-0 record that month. And not only that, she was also named to the 2018 NWSL Best XI, solidifying her place among the league's elite. Though. Like any top athlete, Lindsey had her fair share of bumps along the way. She dealt with injuries, the mental toll of balancing club and international duties, and the constant pressure to perform at the highest level. But even in the rough patches, she kept moving forward. Take 2020, for instance. That was the year of the pandemic, and while most sports leagues came to a halt, the NWSL found a way to make it work with the Fall Series and the NWSL Challenge Cup. Lindsey? Oh, she played a *key* role in leading the Thorns to success in both tournaments. Portland won the Fall Series, taking home the NWSL Community Shield, and then went on to win the Challenge Cup in 2021. It was yet another testament to her leadership and resilience.

And speaking of resilience, how about those 2021 international tournaments? Let's take a minute to talk about Lindsey's performance on the global stage. The USWNT was still riding high off their 2019 World Cup win, and while the Tokyo 2020 Olympics didn't go as planned (delayed due to the pandemic, obviously), Lindsey's performance was still standout. She earned her 100th cap during the Olympics, scoring in a 6-1 victory over New Zealand. That milestone? A reminder that she was now part of an exclusive club of American players who had reached the century mark in international appearances. But again, it wasn't just about the goals—it was about the heart she brought to the game. Even in tough times, like when the USWNT didn't reach the gold medal match, Lindsey was a constant source of fight and passion. By 2022, Portland continued to be Lindsey's home turf, and though the team faced ups and downs, she was a consistent rock for them. That year, Portland Thorns permanently transferred Horan to Lyon in France, closing a chapter that had been filled with championships, MVP titles, and unforgettable moments. But as always with Lindsey, she was ready for the next challenge.

So, what do we take away from Lindsey Horan's Portland years? That she's a leader, a warrior, and someone who knows how to rise to the occasion when her team needs her most. Whether it's scoring that game-winning goal in a championship match or guiding younger players to greatness, Lindsey has cemented her place as one of the most influential figures in American women's soccer. But we're not done yet. Because just as Lindsey was leaving Portland, another chapter was starting to unfold—the return to Europe, but this time, on her own terms.

So, Portland was where Lindsey Horan solidified her reputation, right? She built something iconic there. MVP titles, championship trophies, and that no-nonsense leadership style—she became a household name in American soccer. But you know Lindsey by now: she doesn't stay in one place for long if she senses an opportunity to push herself even further. And that next opportunity? A return to Europe, where it had all begun. But this time, it wasn't about proving herself. This time, Lindsey was in control.

In January 2022, Lindsey packed her bags and flew across the Atlantic once again, not to Paris but to Lyon, one of the biggest powerhouses in women's soccer. Lyon Féminin had built a reputation as one of the most dominant teams in Europe, with multiple Champions League trophies to their name. When Lindsey joined on loan, the expectation was simple: win. And win *big*. She wasn't a naive teenager this time; she knew what she was getting into and, more importantly, who she was as a player. Lyon was a chance to write a new chapter in her European career—a chance to return to the continent where she'd faced adversity and come back with her own terms of success. The moment Lindsey stepped into Lyon's training grounds, you could feel it. There was something in the air. She was walking into a squad filled with some of the best players in the world. You had the likes of Wendie Renard, Ada Hegerberg, and Amandine Henry—names that strike fear into opponents but, more than that, demand excellence from their teammates. For a player like Lindsey, this was where she wanted to be, playing against and alongside the best.

And Lyon didn't disappoint. It didn't take long before Lindsey was in the thick of things, bossing the midfield like she had been born for this. Lyon? They were stacking trophies left and right. During Lindsey's time, they won the Division 1 Féminine title twice, added a Coupe de France Féminine trophy, and most importantly—yeah, you guessed it—they lifted the UEFA Women's Champions League trophy in 2022. And here's the kicker: Lindsey was a *key* part of that success. She wasn't just a benchwarmer or a fill-in. She was right there in the trenches, playing in the biggest matches, contributing not only with her playmaking skills but with her sheer ability to read the game. Remember, this was the same Lindsey who once had a rough go of things at PSG. This time, she was winning trophies on her own terms. Oh, and fun fact? After that Champions League victory, she was seen crying on the field like a baby. Not out of sadness, but pure joy. It's moments like that, where you realize how much the journey means to her.

By June 2023, Lindsey had signed a permanent contract in Lyon, keeping her at the club through 2026. And honestly, It was the right move. The French club was the perfect place for her to continue growing. Plus, they didn't train on synthetic turf—a *huge* bonus for Lindsey, whose body didn't fell in love with the synthetic pitches in Portland. So yeah, she was thriving physically and mentally in Lyon. She even celebrated her first hat-trick for the club later in 2023. If there were any doubts about her ability to dominate in Europe, that hat-trick shut them down real quick. But even with all this success at the club level, Lindsey's focus was never far from the U.S. Women's National Team. After all, she had unfinished business—there was still more glory to chase. Remember Tokyo 2020? The USWNT had walked away with a bronze medal, but that wasn't the color they wanted. For a player like Lindsey, who thrives on winning, that third-place finish left a sour taste. And it wasn't just her. The entire squad was itching for redemption, with the 2024 Paris Olympics looming on the horizon. The gold medal was the prize, and they were determined to get it.

When Lindsey walked into the Paris Olympics in 2024, things were different. She wasn't just another player hoping to contribute. She was the captain. Emma Hayes had taken over as head coach, and while some might have expected changes, Hayes stuck with Lindsey as the team's leader, a clear sign of the faith she had in her co-captain. Alongside Alex Morgan, Lindsey wasn't simply tasked with leading on the pitch—she had to guide the team through the pressures of redemption. And let's face it, after the disappointment of the 2023 FIFA World Cup, there was a lot of pressure. But… as usual… Lindsey thrives under pressure. It's practically her natural habitat. The tournament itself was no cakewalk either. The USWNT had to fight tooth and nail through every match. There were the extra-time battles against Japan and Germany in the quarterfinal and semifinal, where Lindsey's leadership, once again, made the difference. She wasn't necessarily scoring all the goals, but she was the engine, keeping the team together when things got tough, making the passes that turned into goal-scoring opportunities, and showing that steely determination that had become her trademark.

Then came the final. It was a dream scenario for a soccer fan—USA vs. Brazil. Marta, one of the greatest players of all time, was leading the charge for Brazil. The entire world tuned in to watch. But this wasn't a match where Brazil was going to have their way. Lindsey Horan and her squad had other plans. In a tight, nervy 1-0 victory, Mallory Swanson (yeah, she's still crushing it too) scored the only goal, giving the U.S. their fifth Olympic gold in women's soccer. And standing there, holding that gold medal with her teammates, Lindsey knew this was one of the coolest moments of her life. All those years of sacrifice, the struggles in Paris, the rise in Portland, and now? Olympic gold!!

Lindsey was quick to credit her teammates, saying, "My teammates made it very easy for me [to lead]." That's the kind of leader she is. She knows that no matter how great a player you are, it's the team that gets you across the finish line. And with Emma Hayes at the helm and a young, vibrant squad around her, Lindsey couldn't help but look toward the future with excitement. This wasn't just the end of a journey—it was the start of something even bigger. With the 2027 World Cup on the horizon, she knew this team had *so* much more to give. Lindsey's Olympic win was a culmination of everything she'd been through. It was a nod to the sacrifices, the tough days at PSG, the leadership growth in Portland, and the triumphant return to Europe. It was proof that she could lead a team to victory on the world's biggest stages and that she could inspire the next generation of players in ways she never thought possible when she was just a girl from Golden, Colorado, who skipped college to play soccer in Paris.

At 30, Lindsey Horan had become more than a soccer player. She was a trailblazer. She was a captain. She was, in every sense of the word, a champion. And while her eyes were firmly on the future, you know she wasn't done yet. If you thought this was the pinnacle? Nah, Lindsey's got more in store. The 2027 World Cup is just around the corner, and something tells me she's going to be ready—maybe even more than ever.

Brittney Griner

"Tallest, Toughest, Unstoppable" ... The Basketball Star Who Overcame It All

Brittney Griner started her adventure in the world on October 18, 1990, right in the heart of Houston! She started life in a way that would seem familiar to many. She was the youngest of four children, Brittney's dad, Raymond Griner, was a brave deputy sheriff and a hero from the Vietnam War, and her mom's name is Sandra. But while her family was typical in many ways, Brittney herself was anything but. From a young age, she was tall—like, *really* tall. It wasn't the kind of height that people missed or brushed off. Even by elementary school, Brittney stood out, a fact she'd continue to grapple with well into her teen years. It's one thing to be tall, but it's another thing entirely to be *6'9"* by the time you're in high school.

Being *different*—especially in a world that prizes conformity—meant that Brittney faced a lot of unnecessary negativity. There were constant whispers, people questioning if she was even a girl. "People are either going to accept me for who I am, or they're not," Brittney would later say, a sentiment that was forged from years of enduring comments like, "Oh, she's not a female; she's a male," or experiencing moments where kids would touch her chest to mock her. It wasn't easy, and at times it was downright soul-crushing. But Brittney had a secret weapon—resilience. This mental toughness would become her cornerstone as she pushed forward, refusing to let the world's narrow opinions confine her. Let's be real—middle school and high school can be pretty tough for everyone, let alone someone who feels out of place every day. By 7th grade, Brittney's isolation and sadness could have derailed her entirely. "I've had moments when I questioned my place in the world," she admitted, reflecting on those tough adolescent years. But even in those dark times, something inside her wouldn't let her give up. Instead, she embraced what made her *different*. She pushed herself to be Brittney without saying sorry. And that's when basketball showed up.

Brittney attended Nimitz High School in Houston, Texas, where her towering height became less of a burden and more of an advantage. Basketball gave her something to focus on, a place where being tall was not just okay—it was awesome! As a freshman, she also played varsity volleyball, showing off her versatility. But it was during her sophomore year that she began honing her skills in basketball, practicing alongside the boys' team to develop her strength and technique. It was here that Brittney started working with the football coach to develop her leg strength and, most notably, practice dunking—something almost unheard of in women's basketball at the time. This hard work really paid off. The summer before her junior year, a video of Brittney dunking started circulating on YouTube, eventually racking up over *6.6 million views*. Her life changed in a blink. She changed from being the tall girl who felt out of place to becoming super popular and loved by everyone!. Suddenly, everyone wanted to meet this girl who could dunk like the NBA's best players. And one day, she got a surprise that even she couldn't have imagined—*Shaquille O'Neal* wanted to meet her. Imagine that: one of the greatest big men to ever play basketball, a legend in his own right, sitting down with a high schooler from Houston. And Brittney *earned* it.

Even though she became really popular, Brittney still faced a lot of challenges in high school. She was playing on a stage larger than most high school athletes ever experience, and with that came pressure. During her junior season, Brittney led the Nimitz Cougars to the Texas 5A Girls Basketball State Championship game. They were close—so close—but fell short, losing 52-43 to Mansfield Summit High School. In that game, Brittney dunked, setting a record for *seven dunks* in a single game. It's game-changing. She had dunked a total of *52 times* across 32 games in her senior year alone, completely transforming the image of what was possible in women's high school basketball. And it wasn't just her scoring that got noticed.—Brittney's defense was super strong! In one game against Houston Alief Hastings, she blocked *25 shots*, the most ever recorded by a female high school player in the U.S. This was history in the making. She ended her senior season with an astonishing 318 blocks, setting a new single-season record.

Everyone saw how amazing she was in high school! By 2009, Brittney was named the *nation's No. 1 high school women's basketball player* by Rivals.com and a McDonald's All-American, the highest honor a high school basketball player can achieve. Houston's mayor even declared May 7, 2009, *Brittney Griner Day* in her honor. That year, she also participated in the WBCA High School All-America Game, where she led her team with *20 points and 9 rebounds*. But even with her growing fame, things weren't always easy... Being different, especially when you're young, can make you feel alone. She talked about the sadness and anger she felt at times, the loneliness of standing out when all she wanted was to fit in. Yet, instead of allowing the negativity to break her down, Brittney found a way to channel it into her game. Basketball was her way to prove everyone wrong and, more importantly, to prove to *herself* that she belonged. She developed a fierce mentality, understanding that people were either going to accept her or not. And to be honest, If they weren't going to like her for who she was, she didn't need their okay.

Basketball became Brittney's ticket to rise above all the noise, all the doubts, and all the criticisms thrown her way. Every block, every dunk, every game became a statement. She wasn't just playing to win; she was playing to change the game completely! In high school, Brittney's story was already one of triumph, even though she was just starting on what she would achieve later. But her resilience, her ability to withstand and grow from hard times, was cemented in these early years. And the world had only begun to see the force that Brittney Griner was becoming.

Brittney Griner's move from high school star to college basketball icon was like going from one amazing world to a whole new level of awesome! Her arrival at *Baylor University* in 2009 was the moment when Brittney would truly begin to shape the future of women's basketball. Standing at 6'9" tall, with arms so long they reach an incredible 87.5 inches across! Griner was about to dominate in ways the game had never seen before. But the thing is, it wasn't only her physicality that made Brittney a force of nature; it was the mindset she had been building since her early days in Houston—the unstoppable drive to show she belonged, to rise above any doubts, and to change what everyone thought was possible in the game.

As a *freshman* at Baylor, Brittney quickly made her mark on the court. That season, she blocked *223 shots*—setting an all-time NCAA single-season record. And those blocks weren't just to boost her stats; they were bold statements, a warning to anyone who dared drive to the basket: Brittney Griner was waiting. On December 16, 2009, Brittney recorded *Baylor's first-ever triple-double*, racking up 34 points, 13 rebounds, and a *Big 12 Conference record 11 blocked shots* in one game. Let that sink in—she wasn't just scoring or rebounding; she was shutting teams down, one block at a time, on a level no one had seen before. Brittney was more than a player—she was a game-changer...

By the time March rolled around, it became crystal clear that Baylor had something special. In the *2010 NCAA Tournament*, Brittney led the charge, and in a Sweet 16 matchup against top-seeded Tennessee, the world witnessed something historic. Brittney *blocked 14 shots* in a single game—an NCAA Tournament record. That same tournament, in a nail-biter against Duke, she added *9 more blocks*, breaking the overall tournament record for most blocks, finishing with *35 blocks* in total. Brittney was rewriting the record books while doing it. But as always, the game wasn't always easy... College brought its own set of personal and professional challenges. One of the biggest moments in her career that got people talking happened in March 2010, during a heated game against Texas Tech. Brittney and an opponent, Jordan Barncastle, were jostling for position when things escalated—Brittney, frustrated, threw a punch that broke Barncastle's nose. It was a mistake, no doubt, and Brittney was ejected from the game. Her coach, *Kim Mulkey*, imposed an additional one-game suspension, on top of the one mandated by the NCAA. It was a low point for Brittney, a moment that could have defined her negatively. But instead of letting that mistake tarnish her reputation, she used it as a stepping stone—a lesson learned in the heat of battle, a moment to grow from rather than shrink under. And grow she did.

The following season, in *2010-2011*, Brittney was determined to prove that she was more than her mistakes. Scoring an average of 23 points per game during their second year, she continued to evolve, leading Baylor through another deep run in the NCAA Tournament. In a career-high performance during the Sweet 16, Brittney dropped *40 points* on Green Bay, proving that when it mattered most, she could take over a game, not just defensively, but offensively, too. And while Baylor's season ended with a tough loss to eventual champions, *Texas A&M*, Brittney was already setting the stage for an even greater comeback.

In her *junior year*, everything clicked. Brittney Griner was unstoppable. Averaging *23.2 points*, *9.4 rebounds*, and a mind-blowing *5 blocks per game*, she was blocking more shots than most *entire teams* in Division I. Baylor went on a tear that season, winning game after game, and heading into the 2012 NCAA Tournament, expectations were sky-high. Brittney didn't disappoint. In the National Championship game against Notre Dame, she delivered one of the most dominant performances in the history of women's college basketball. Baylor won the championship with an *80-61* victory, with Brittney scoring *26 points*, grabbing *13 rebounds*, and blocking *5 shots*. She was named the *Most Outstanding Player of the Final Four*, solidifying her place in NCAA history. But it wasn't just about the championship; that season, Baylor finished *40-0*, the first and *only team* to ever achieve that feat in NCAA history.

By the time her junior season ended, Brittney had accumulated so many accolades that it became hard to keep track of them all. She was named the *AP Player of the Year* and *Naismith College Player of the Year*, both of which she would win again during her *senior year*. She also received the prestigious *Honda Sports Award* in 2012, and to cap it all off, Brittney was honored with the *Wade Trophy*, given to the best NCAA Division I player who exemplifies the spirit of Margaret Wade. All eyes were on Brittney as she secured her spot as the best women's college basketball player in the nation. Yet despite all the success,

Brittney remained grounded. "I think I can be great," she once said, but never in a way that suggested she believed she had already arrived. She was constantly evolving, always pushing for more.

Her final year at Baylor wasn't without setbacks. Going into her *senior season*, the expectations were astronomical. Brittney and Baylor were poised to repeat as national champions. In many ways, she didn't disappoint. Averaging *23.8 points, 9.4 rebounds,* and *4.1 blocks per game,* she continued to dominate. Baylor reached the Sweet 16, but in a shocking upset, they lost to Louisville, ending Brittney's college career sooner than anyone expected. It was a tough pill to swallow, but by then, Brittney had already etched her name among the greatest to ever play the game.

Throughout her four years at Baylor, Brittney compiled a jaw-dropping *135-15* record, securing three Big 12 Conference regular season titles and three Big 12 Tournament championships. On top of that, she left Baylor as the all-time *NCAA leader in blocks—748* blocks to be exact—and finished third all-time in points scored, with *3,283*. Let that number sink in—*3,283 points*. Not only was Brittney the most dominant defensive player the women's game had ever seen, but she was also an offensive juggernaut. Brittney Griner also changed the way people thought about women's basketball. Before her, dunking in women's basketball was extremely rare.—something that happened once in a blue moon. By the time Brittney left Baylor, she had dunked *18 times* in her college career, more than any player in women's NCAA history, and each slam was a message, A glimpse of what the future of women's basketball could look like.

In many ways, Brittney's college career was the ultimate display of resilience and mental toughness. From the challenges of her freshman year to the growing pains of learning to handle hard times, from the pressure of national expectations to the personal journey of learning to manage her emotions on the court, Brittney's journey was one of constant evolution. Baylor was more than just a place where she played basketball; it was where she transformed into a symbol of perseverance and an icon for the next generation of players. Every block, every dunk, every moment of triumph was a response to those who doubted her, who made her feel like an outsider. But rather than break under the pressure, Brittney rose above it, turning every challenge into fuel. She showed that it wasn't just about winning; it was about *how* you win—how you face hard times and how you rise again, even when the odds seem stacked against you.

After a record-shattering college career at Baylor, Brittney Griner was ready to take on the world—and the world was *definitely* ready for her. In 2013, Brittney entered the WNBA Draft, and it was no surprise that she was selected as the *first overall pick* by the *Phoenix Mercury*. Her journey from the courts of Houston and Baylor had brought her to the *big leagues*, and everyone was eager to see what the 6'9" phenom would do next. In her *debut game* on May 27, 2013, against the Chicago Sky, Brittney *dunked twice*, tying the WNBA dunk record set by Candace Parker. And that was just her first game. Her shot-blocking ability—which had become legendary in college—translated seamlessly into the pros. Griner quickly became amazing at defense, leading her league with an average of 3 blocks in every game of her first season. Unfortunately, a knee injury kept her from playing in the 2013 WNBA All-Star Game, but she was still named an All-Star—a title she would earn many more times.

In 2014, Griner took her game to new heights. With an average of *15.6 points*, *8.0 rebounds*, and an otherworldly *3.7 blocks per game*, she was a *two-way force* unlike anything the WNBA had ever seen. The Phoenix Mercury, with Griner anchoring the defense and her dynamic teammates Diana Taurasi and Candice Dupree handling the offense, put together one of the best seasons in WNBA history. They finished with a 29-5 record, setting the WNBA record for most wins in a season. Brittney's incredible skill shone brightest in the WNBA Finals, where she led the Mercury to sweep the Chicago Sky in three games. She also broke records with the most blocks in a finals game (8) and the most in a single quarter (5), showcasing her unmatched presence on the court. That 2014 season earned her her *first WNBA Championship*, and she was just getting started. Defensively, Brittney was on another planet. In 2015, despite missing seven games, she averaged a *career-high* and WNBA-record *4.0 blocks per game*, surpassing the previous record set by Margo Dydek in 1998. In one playoff game against the Tulsa Shock, Brittney delivered an *11-block performance*—setting a playoff record and sending a clear message: anyone driving into the lane against her did so at their own risk. Her talents took her *around the globe*. During the WNBA off-seasons, Griner played overseas in China and Russia, where she earned more in a few months than she did during the entire WNBA season. While playing for *UMMC Ekaterinburg* in Russia, Brittney won four big championships in Europe, showing she's one of the best basketball players in the whole world! And let's not forget her time in China... Brittney's amazing dunks and super strong defense helped her teams go far in the playoffs. No matter where she played, Brittney Griner was always the biggest star on the court—both by how tall she is and how great she plays!

By 2016, Brittney had already created an amazing legacy, but her biggest stage was still to come: the *Olympics*.

That year, Brittney was selected to represent Team USA in the *Rio de Janeiro Summer Olympics*, and she delivered in typical Griner fashion. Averaging 9.3 points and 5.6 rebounds during the games, Brittney helped Team USA zoom to a gold medal, winning with a whopping score of 101-72 against Spain in the big final! It was her *first Olympic gold*, but definitely not her last. Brittney joined an elite group of players who have won an NCAA title, a WNBA Championship, and an Olympic gold medal—proving that her talents transcended every level of basketball.

Brittney's dominance on the court continued year after year, earning her accolades like *Defensive Player of the Year* twice (2014, 2015) and being named a *WNBA All-Star* a whopping *10 times*. In 2017, she re-signed with the Phoenix Mercury on a multi-year deal and rewarded them with her *best offensive season to date*, averaging *21.9 points per game* and leading the league in scoring while also leading the league in blocks for the *fifth consecutive season*. That year, she dropped a career-high *38 points* in an overtime win against the Indiana Fever, showing that while she was known for her defense, she could absolutely take over a game offensively when needed.

Comes 2022, when life had one of its toughest bumpy rides for Brittney... her career came to an abrupt halt when she was detained in Russia on charges of drug smuggling after less than a gram of hash oil—medically prescribed—was found in her luggage. The news stunned everyone. Brittney was given a nine-year sentence in a Russian penal colony, a decision that seemed unbelievable... For nearly *300 days*, Brittney faced incredible difficulties in a foreign prison, sparking an international movement to secure her release. U.S. officials, calling her detention "wrongful," worked tirelessly to bring Brittney home. On December 8, 2022, everyone heard the news they had been hoping for—Brittney Griner was released in a swap for Russian arms dealer Viktor Bout. The moment she stepped back onto American soil, Brittney's life and career began a brand new chapter!

Her comeback to the WNBA in 2023 was truly heroic! Despite the emotional and physical toll of her time in prison in Russia, Brittney played 31 of 40 games for the Phoenix Mercury, averaging *17.5 points* and *6.3 rebounds* per game. Wherever she played, fans stood up and cheered for her, celebrating her awesome basketball skills and the strong spirit she showed coming back even better after almost a year of tough times. And guess what... Brittney wasn't done yet. Off the court, Brittney started using her platform to speak up for people who were wrongfully detained in other countries. She dedicated herself to using her experience to highlight the struggles of others in similar tough situations. Brittney's newfound voice in the world of social justice made her more than just an athlete—she became a symbol of resilience, a figure who had survived unimaginable challenges and returned determined to make the world a better place!

But basketball was still Brittney's passion, and she wasn't going to let her time away from the game shape who she was. In *2024*, Brittney was selected to represent Team USA once again at the *Paris Summer Olympics*. She was now a seasoned veteran, having won gold in 2016 and 2020 (Tokyo Olympics, held in 2021). And just as she had in the past, Brittney came through when it mattered most. In the gold medal game, Team USA faced off against France in a hard-fought battle that went down to the wire. Brittney contributed *four crucial points* and provided the kind of defensive presence that only she could, helping Team USA secure a dramatic *67-66* victory over France to win their *eighth consecutive gold medal !!*

For Brittney, snagging her third Olympic gold medal wasn't just a personal victory—it was a big, shiny shout-out to her toughness, bounce-back spirit, and knack for leaping over hurdles! In her own words, she once said, "You can't control injuries, but you can control how hard you work to come back." And come back she did. Every setback, every hurdle Brittney faced, from the toughest games to the darkest moments of her life, only made her stronger... With her *third Olympic gold* in hand. Whether she's wowing everyone with her awesome dunks or helping others, Brittney has shown that being strong in your mind and heart can help you beat any tough stuff that comes your way.

Sydney McLaughlin-Levrone

"SHATTERING LIMITS"
... THE QUEEN WHO TURNS HURDLES INTO HISTORY

In a small corner of New Jersey, Sydney McLaughlin-Levrone grew up in a house where running was a *very* serious business. In fact, rumor has it that her family didn't walk anywhere—they sprinted. They raced to the fridge, dashed to the TV remote, and you can bet they had hurdles lined up in the hallway just to keep things interesting. Born on August 7, 1999, in New Brunswick, Sydney was the third child in a family where running was basically their version of brushing teeth. Her dad, Willie, was no slouch—he was practically a track superstar himself, a three-time All-American who ran so fast he almost made the U.S. Olympic team in 1984. He could've been rocking gold medals at the Olympics if a few seconds hadn't gotten in his way. But hold up, because her mom, Mary, wasn't about to let her husband hog all the track glory. She was out there running, too. In fact, back when she was in high school, Mary ran on the *boys'* team because, believe it or not, her school didn't have a track team for girls. She was fast enough to keep up with the boys—let's be honest, probably faster than half of them—and ran the 800 meters like it was no big deal. When Mary and Willie met in college at Manhattan College, they bonded over their mutual love of running and became the fastest couple in all of New Jersey (or at least that's how I like to imagine it haha). Fast-forward a few years and BOOM! Sydney was born—*already* destined to wear out more pairs of sneakers than most people wear socks.

Growing up in Dunellen, New Jersey, Sydney had siblings who could've started their own track team. There was Taylor, Morgan, and little Ryan—each one faster than the next, it seemed... Taylor, her older brother, was basically a superstar in his own right. He even won a silver medal in the 400-meter hurdles at the 2016 IAAF World U20 Championships. Sydney looked up to him like he was a real-life superhero in spikes. But let's get real for a second: Taylor probably wasn't always a superhero. Like all older brothers, he probably had his moments of being annoying, maybe hogging the TV remote after his sprints to the couch or racing Sydney for the last slice of pizza. Still, Sydney followed in his speedy footsteps—though she was *determined* to leave him and the rest of her family in the dust one day.

At age *14*, Sydney already had people turning their heads, not because she wore neon-colored sneakers (though that would've been cool too), but because she was *fast*. No—she was *crazy fast*. When most kids were trying to figure out the perfect way to sneak their vegetables to the family dog, Sydney was out there breaking world records for her age group. In 2014, at the National Junior Championships, she came in second place behind a girl who was, well, pretty legendary herself—Shamier Little. But that didn't stop Sydney from making history. Her time of 55.63 seconds in the 400-meter hurdles was the fastest ever for a 14-year-old, not just in New Jersey, but in *the entire world*! If there was a gold medal for best 14-year-old ever at running the 400-meter hurdles, it would've been hanging around her neck faster than you can say "pass the baton."... The crazy thing is, she *almost* made it to the 2014 World Junior Championships, but she was too young by one year. ONE YEAR! Can you imagine? Like, she was *too good* for her own age. She was running so fast that the world had to hit pause and say, "Whoa, whoa, let's give the other kids a chance to catch up." But that's not all. Oh no, Sydney wasn't about to stop at one event. That same year, she set another world record in the 100-meter hurdles for her age group, like it was a casual weekend activity. *Who does that?* Most kids were lucky to win a school race, but Sydney? She was busy winning on the world stage before she even had a driver's license.

At home, her parents had already gotten used to having their kids' names plastered on every track record book in the area. But even they were starting to realize that Sydney was *something else*. Her dad, Willie, was always telling anyone who would listen, "All of our kids are talented, but Sydney's a little special." No kidding, Willie! Sydney wasn't just a little special; she was on track to becoming the fastest McLaughlin in the house—maybe the fastest in the world?

Sydney's life was all about balance. And by balance, I mean balancing running fast and doing normal kid stuff. Because when she wasn't out there breaking records, she was a regular student at Union Catholic Regional High School in Scotch Plains. Well, *regular* might be a stretch. She became the first *two-time* Gatorade Player of the Year in track and field. Yes, two-time. That's like being crowned King or Queen of the Track, *twice*, and they didn't even have to invent a new crown for her. Let's not forget her siblings, though. They were all busy racing, too—Taylor at the University of Michigan, Morgan at St. Peter's University, and little Ryan, who was following closely behind like, "Don't forget about me!" In fact, Ryan was the *fifth* McLaughlin to win a New Jersey county track title, making it clear that if you had the last name McLaughlin, you were practically required to win at least one race in your lifetime.

So there was Sydney, with her track-star siblings, her speedy parents, and her house full of sneakers—seriously, they probably had more sneakers than they knew what to do with. And though she was already dominating on the track, Sydney was still just a high schooler, trying to make it through algebra class like everybody else. Except, unlike everybody else, she was also making history every time she laced up her shoes.

By the time Sydney McLaughlin entered Union Catholic Regional High School, it was pretty obvious she wasn't just your regular high school freshman. Most freshmen are trying to figure out how to open their lockers, but Sydney? She was already figuring out how to *crush* records on the track—and we're not talking about your average school records. No, Sydney was breaking *world* records. It's like she came to high school with her own superhero cape, except instead of a cape, she had a stopwatch that kept gasping, "Did she really just run that fast?!". Union Catholic had probably never seen a kid like Sydney before. Most kids brought their lunch in a brown bag; Sydney probably carried hers in a gold medal box (okay, not true, but close). She walked through the halls like an undercover superhero, one who quietly aced tests and then sprinted out to practice to casually set records like it was no big deal. On top of all that, she had this superpower of balancing everything—training, homework, and, oh, you know, being the fastest high school runner anyone had ever seen.

Let's rewind to 2014, her freshman year. That was the year when Sydney first made people drop their jaws, spill their Gatorade, and ask, "Wait, how *old* is she?!" At the National Junior Championships, Sydney lined up for the 400-meter hurdles like she was just some regular 14-year-old kid. But no. She wasn't regular. She wasn't *anywhere* close to regular. She crossed the finish line in 55.63 seconds, which, for the record, is faster than most people can say, "Wow, she's fast!" That time was a national high school *freshman* record, a world *age-14* best, and would've probably gotten her into the World Junior Championships—except, oops, she was too young by one measly year. Can you imagine being *too fast* for your age group? It's like when you try to ride a roller coaster, and they're like, "Sorry, kid, you're too short," but in Sydney's case, it was, "Sorry, kid, you're too fast. Maybe next year." So she took her 55.63-second victory lap home and said, "No problem, I'll just be faster next time." And she was.

But here's where things get crazy. While most kids were celebrating their summer with, I don't know, sleepovers or pool parties, Sydney spent her summer smashing records. That same year, she also clocked a time of 13.34 seconds in the 100-meter hurdles, setting another world age-group best. If there was a record out there, you can bet Sydney was coming for it. She didn't just want to win races—she wanted to *obliterate* records. It was like she had a checklist at home: Get good grades, break a world record, eat dinner, go to bed. Casual...

So, fast forward to 2015. Sydney is now a sophomore, but let's be real: she was running like a *pro*. That year, she ran the 400-meter hurdles at the national youth trials and won with a time of 55.28 seconds. Not only was that the fastest time for any 15-year-old in the world, but it was also the second-fastest time in the history of youth records, right behind some legendary runner named Leslie Maxie, who set the bar *way* back in 1984. And what did Sydney do after that? Oh, you know, she *flew* to Cali, Colombia, and casually won gold at the World Youth Championships with a time of 55.94 seconds. No big deal. Just another world title for a teenager who probably still had to ask permission to stay out past 9 p.m.

But as incredible as that sounds, let's talk about what happened next—because, honestly, Sydney wasn't about to slow down. It's like she had turbo-boosters on her sneakers or something. In 2016, she showed up at the New Balance National Outdoor High School Championships ready to *destroy* everything in her path. She sprinted her way through the 400-meter hurdles in 54.46 seconds, breaking not just one, but *three* records in the process. She smashed Leslie Maxie's 32-year-old high school record, shattered Lashinda Demus's American junior record, and left everyone asking, "How is she still in high school?!" ... Oh, and then, as if that wasn't enough, she also ran a 50.93-second split in the Swedish medley relay. (Which, in case you're wondering, is not a race where they hand off meatballs, but it's actually a relay with different distances for each runner.) Sydney and her Union Catholic teammates set a new high school record in the event. And just because she was in a record-smashing mood, she also helped her team break a high school record for the 4x400 relay, clocking a time of 3:38.92. Her split? A blistering 50.37 seconds. The crowd? Left completely speechless. Her sneakers? Probably *melting* from the sheer speed.

But hold onto your hats, because the summer of 2016 was *the* summer that Sydney went from "high school phenom" to "the kid who might just go to the *Olympics* before she even graduates." At the U.S. Olympic Trials that year, Sydney lined up for the 400-meter hurdles—no pressure or anything—and guess what? She placed *third*. THIRD. Do you know what that means? It means she officially qualified for the Olympics in Rio de Janeiro. She wasn't even done with high school yet, and she was already packing her bags for the *Olympics*. And how did she do it? Well, she set another world youth best with a time of 54.15 seconds. Because, of course, she did.

Now, I know what you're thinking: "She's probably too young to handle the pressure of the Olympic Games, right?". Sydney showed up in Rio like she had been there a million times before, totally unphased by the fact that she was competing against grown adults from around the world. She made it all the way to the semi-finals, where she placed fifth in her heat. Sure, she didn't make the finals, but come on—*she was 16*! While most kids were worrying about their junior prom, Sydney was running circles around the best athletes on the planet.

By now, Sydney's high school career was practically legendary. She became the first two-time Gatorade National Girls Athlete of the Year, which is like winning the track-and-field version of the Oscars. And just in case you needed any more proof that she was officially the biggest deal in high school athletics, she landed on the cover of *Sports Illustrated* in 2017, her senior year. That's right—*Sports Illustrated*. The magazine even called her "one of the most dominant high school athletes ever," which is probably the understatement of the century. I mean, *duh*, she was practically a high school superhero with a speedometer for a heartbeat. But before she could hang up her high school spikes, Sydney had *one more* historic race left in her. At the New Balance Outdoor Nationals in 2017, she took the baton in *sixth* place during the 4x400 relay. The crowd might have been biting their nails, wondering if Union Catholic could even make it to the podium. But Sydney? Sydney was probably just thinking, "No biggie, I'll just pass *five teams* on my way to victory." And that's exactly what she did. She ran her leg in 49.85 seconds, leaving the competition in the dust and leading her team to a come-from-behind victory. Mic drop.

And with that, Sydney's high school chapter closed with more records than most people collect in a lifetime. She left Union Catholic as the greatest thing to ever happen to high school track—and probably the *fastest* thing too. But the world wasn't ready for what came next, because Sydney was about to take her talents to *college*, where the speedometer was about to break all over again.

After Sydney McLaughlin-Levrone wrapped up her *mind-blowing* high school career—leaving behind a trail of melted spikes, broken records, and jaws permanently dropped—it was time for her next adventure: *college*. But not just any college. In 2017, Sydney signed a National Letter of Intent to attend the University of Kentucky, where she planned to keep doing what she did best—running so fast that the speed of sound got jealous. Now, before we go any further, let's get one thing clear: Sydney didn't *need* to go to college to prove herself. She had already been to the Olympics as a high schooler! But, like any hero on a mission, Sydney knew she could still push herself to new limits. So, off she went to Kentucky, ready to turn the college track world upside down—and she wasted no time doing just that.

At the 2018 NCAA Division I Indoor Track and Field Championships, Sydney went ahead and set a *world junior record* with a time of 50.36 seconds on 400 meters. You know, as one does. And then, because breaking *one* record wasn't nearly enough, she stepped outside in May 2018 for her first SEC Championship appearance and shattered the *collegiate* record in the 400-meter hurdles, finishing in 52.75 seconds. I mean, come on. By this point, Sydney was treating records like piñatas at a birthday party. One swing—BOOM—new record. Another swing—BOOM—another record. Her time at Kentucky was short but *legendary*.

But then came the big decision. In June 2018, Sydney decided to go pro. That's right—she traded in her Wildcats jersey for a *professional* contract with New Balance. And if you thought she was fast before, wait until you hear what happened next. With legendary coach Bob Kersee by her side—this guy's basically the Gandalf of track and field—Sydney was ready to take on the *entire* world. No joke.

Now let's fast forward a little to the year 2019. Sydney stepped onto the world stage once again at the IAAF World Championships in Doha, Qatar, ready to show the world that her high school and college heroics were just the beginning. But standing in her way was another track legend, Dalilah Muhammad, the reigning Olympic gold medalist. In one of the most epic races ever, Sydney gave it her all, finishing with a personal best time of 52.23 seconds. But here's the thing—Dalilah beat her by a *teeny-tiny* 0.07 seconds. It was *that* close. So, while Sydney didn't win gold, she still walked away with a shiny silver medal and a new fire in her heart. Oh, and don't worry, she got her revenge soon enough. *Trust me.*

The following year, 2020, came with all kinds of challenges—you know, like the *entire world* shutting down—but that didn't slow Sydney down. If anything, she came out of it *stronger*. By the time the 2021 U.S. Olympic Trials rolled around, Sydney wasn't messing around. She ran the 400-meter hurdles in 51.90 seconds, breaking the *world record*. Yes, you heard that right. She took Dalilah Muhammad's world record and said, "Thanks, I'll be keeping this one." And then, she packed her bags for Tokyo.

In Tokyo, she and Dalilah Muhammad lined up for another epic showdown in the 400-meter hurdles. The world held its breath. Would Sydney break the record again? Would Dalilah defend her title? Would anyone's shoes survive this race? As it turns out, Sydney didn't just break the record; she *obliterated* it. She ran the 400-meter hurdles in 51.46 seconds, a time so fast it left the commentators gasping for air. Sydney was officially a gold medalist, and she wasn't done yet.

She then joined Team USA for the 4x400 meter relay, running with other superstars like Allyson Felix (who, by the way, probably has more gold medals than a pirate's treasure chest). Together, they *dominated*, winning gold with a time of 3:16.85. Sydney's split was so fast that clocks everywhere had to take a minute to recover. Two gold medals. *Two!* And let's not forget that she was now a double world-record holder. It was the stuff of legends, and Sydney was *just getting started*.

Fast forward to 2022. Sydney wasn't about to let the world forget who she was, so at the World Championships in Eugene, Oregon, she did what she does best: broke her *own* world record. This time, she ran the 400-meter hurdles in 50.68 seconds. Let me say that again for emphasis: *50.68 seconds*. That's a time so fast that most people would need a jetpack to keep up. And, of course, she won another gold medal in the 4x400 meter relay, because at this point, winning gold was practically part of her daily routine. Wake up, brush teeth, win gold.

Let's then talk about the grand finale: the *2024 Paris Olympics*. This is where Sydney really cemented her status as a *legend among legends*. First up was the 400-meter hurdles, her signature event. By now, the world record was *basically* Sydney's personal property. It had her name on it, and she wasn't about to let anyone take it. On August 8, 2024, Sydney stood at the starting line, her eyes locked on the finish line like it was her destiny. The gun went off, and Sydney ran like she was racing against the wind itself. She cleared each hurdle with the kind of grace and speed that made you wonder if she was part superhero. And when she crossed the finish line? She broke the world record *again*. This time, her time was an *unbelievable* 50.37 seconds. That's right—*50.37!* Let that sink in. She shattered the boundaries of what anyone thought was possible. It was her *fourth* world record in just a few years. Oh, and by the way, she's the *only* person in history to break four world records in the same event. Not too shabby, right? But wait... she wasn't done yet. Sydney teamed up with the U.S. squad once again for the 4x400 meter relay, because what's better than one gold medal? Two gold medals, of course. And they crushed it, as usual. Their time of

3:15.27 was the fastest relay time of the year, and Sydney's split? An insane 47.71 seconds. It's like she was racing the *Flash* and winning.

So, there she was—Sydney McLaughlin-Levrone, standing in the middle of the Stade de France, a *four-time* Olympic gold medalist. She had broken world records, won everything there was to win, and left the competition wondering how they'd ever catch up. But if you asked Sydney, she'd tell you there was something *far* more important to her than the medals and the records. She wasn't running for her own glory—she was running for God's. See, throughout all her success, Sydney stayed grounded in her faith. After her epic win in Tokyo, she posted on Instagram, giving all the credit to God. She wrote, "What I have in Christ is far greater than what I have or don't have in life." For Sydney, running was more than just about winning; it was about using the gifts she'd been given to honor something much bigger than herself. She even wrote a book about her journey, called *Far Beyond Gold: Running from Fear to Faith*, where she shared how her faith guided her through every hurdle (literally and metaphorically) in her life.

And when the Paris Olympics were over? Well, Sydney celebrated the way any champion would—by munching on croissants and soaking in the *surreal* feeling of being the greatest hurdler the world had ever seen. The crowd roared, her family cheered, and Sydney? She just smiled, knowing she had given it her all, not for the glory, but for something far greater.

Ryan Crouser

"THE GIANT WHO THREW THE WORLD" ... THE GREATEST SHOT PUT AND DISCUS CHAMPION IN TRACK AND FIELD

What's the deal with Boring, Oregon? I mean, with a name like that, you're not exactly expecting rollercoasters and fireworks, but that's where this story begins. It was a quiet, sleepy place where the most dramatic thing you'd see was someone walking their dog slowly down the road—like really slow, as if even the dog had nothing better to do. But there was something not boring at all happening right there in the countryside. A giant was growing up, one destined to be the strongest in all the land! And this giant went by the name Ryan Crouser.

Now, when I say "giant," I don't mean the stomping, roaring kind you'd read about in some old fairytale—though if you saw Ryan, you'd think he could lift a whole castle with one hand. Standing at a staggering 6 feet 7 inches tall, Ryan didn't blend in with the other kids at school. By the time he was in fifth grade, he was already throwing things further than anyone could believe—probably starting with his homework, but more likely, it was sports equipment. And if you saw how big he was, you'd wonder if he had superpowers, but here's the thing: it wasn't magic; it was family.

See, Ryan Crouser came from a family so full of athletic superstars that they might as well have been superheroes—superheroes who all threw things for a living. His dad, Mitch Crouser, could launch a discus (a heavy, flat, circular object thrown in track and field events) as if he were throwing a frisbee to a dog that was three counties away! In fact, Mitch was so good that he was almost on the U.S. Olympic team in 1984. And guess what, that wasn't even the end of it. Ryan's uncles, Brian and Dean Crouser, were equally legendary. Brian competed in the Olympics twice in the javelin (a long spear thrown in competitions), while Dean was an NCAA champion (the best college athlete) in both the shot put and the discus.

I know what you're thinking: what kind of family competitions must those have been? Thanksgiving at the Crouser house probably wasn't about who could finish their pumpkin pie the fastest; it was more like, "Hey, who can throw this turkey the farthest across the backyard?" And with a competitive family like that, losing was never an option. Even board games weren't safe. "No matter what it is—pick-up basketball in the front yard or touch football... even Monopoly is ridiculous," Ryan once shared, with a grin that told you he knew what he was talking about. "Nobody wants to lose." And in a family like the Crousers, losing was practically forbidden. You had to win at everything, even if it meant you'd been practicing your "game face" (your most serious and focused expression) since you were five years old. So, it's no surprise that young Ryan had some serious competition at home. His cousin Sam was also on his way to becoming an Olympic javelin thrower, and his other cousin Haley was throwing javelins at a high level too—because, you know, that's what Crousers do: they throw things far. It's like they were all born with springs in their arms instead of muscles, giving them extra power to send objects flying.

Ryan's love for throwing things began in a very special place: his grandfather Larry's backyard. Picture it: little Ryan, maybe smaller than he is now but still towering over most kids his age, standing there with his grandpa, who was once a javelin thrower himself. Grandpa Larry wasn't about to let his giant grandson waste his talents on something ordinary like, say, video games. Larry put a shot put (a heavy metal ball used in track and field events) in Ryan's hand and showed him the ropes (taught him how to do it). And Ryan was hooked. "One of the very first times I was throwing, and my grandfather was working with me... I had a two-foot improvement—which in the shot put is huge," Ryan remembered with a twinkle in his eye. Two feet might not seem like much if you're jumping into a pool, but in shot put, that's like launching a spaceship into a new galaxy!

From that day on, young Ryan found himself obsessed with how he could throw things further and further. He was fascinated by the idea that if you just made a small adjustment—getting lower, using your legs more—you could send that ball soaring like a superhero in flight. "That extra two feet came out of my legs," he said. It was almost as if his legs were hiding some secret turbo power that he didn't know about until Grandpa Larry showed him how to unlock it. And so began the legend of Ryan Crouser, the quiet giant from Boring, who spent his childhood chasing that perfect throw. With a family that could practically throw anything over a mountain and a grandpa who kick-started his journey, Ryan was on his way to becoming a legend. And little did he know, Boring was about to be known for something far from boring—it was about to become the birthplace of one of the greatest shot putters.

> IN SHOT PUT, THE GOAL IS TO THROW A HEAVY METAL BALL (CALLED A "SHOT") AS FAR AS YOU CAN. THE ATHLETE STANDS IN A SMALL CIRCLE AND HOLDS THE SHOT AGAINST THEIR NECK. THEY SPIN OR PUSH FORWARD WITH ONE STRONG MOTION TO THROW THE SHOT INTO A MARKED FIELD. THE DISTANCE THE SHOT TRAVELS IS MEASURED, AND THE PERSON WHO THROWS IT THE FARTHEST WINS. IN DISCUS, THE ATHLETE THROWS A FLAT DISC (CALLED A "DISCUS"). LIKE SHOT PUT, THE ATHLETE STANDS IN A CIRCLE AND SPINS QUICKLY TO BUILD UP POWER BEFORE THROWING IT INTO THE FIELD. THE DISTANCE IS MEASURED FROM WHERE THE DISCUS LANDS, AND, AGAIN, THE ATHLETE WHO THROWS IT THE FARTHEST WINS. BOTH SPORTS REQUIRE A LOT OF STRENGTH AND TECHNIQUE TO GET THE MOST DISTANCE ON THE THROW.

So, by the time Ryan Crouser hit high school, he wasn't just that kid who could throw a ball far—he was already a legend in the making. You know how some kids are really good at math, others might be excellent at art, and then there's that one kid who's amazing at sports? Well, Ryan was that kid. Except instead of running or jumping, his sport was hurling enormous objects like they weighed nothing. He was the kind of kid whose backpack probably had to be reinforced with steel just to hold up under the weight of his schoolbooks—because, seriously, this dude was strong.

But here's the twist: despite his family's superhero-like ability to throw things, Ryan didn't just glide through high school with all his athletic ability handed to him on a silver platter (meaning he didn't get everything easily without effort). He worked—and worked hard. Remember, this was a family that didn't mess around. Every throw, every competition was like a mini Olympics for Ryan. And as fate would have it, by the time he was in sophomore year at Sam Barlow High School in Gresham, Oregon, Ryan set a national record for his age group in discus. I mean, he didn't even wait until senior year—he was breaking records before he could drive! He hurled the 1.62 kg (3.58 lb) discus (which is about the weight of a large watermelon) a whopping 61.72 meters (that's more than half a football field!). That distance wasn't just impressive—it was the farthest any kid his age in the entire country had ever thrown. That was farther than most people could throw a crumpled piece of paper across a classroom!

But that's just the start of the magic. You see, once Ryan realized he could be really, really good at this throwing thing, he didn't slow down. Instead, he doubled down—practicing day in and day out, throwing shot puts and discuses like his life depended on it. And because he was Ryan Crouser, each time he'd improve.

In 2009, at just 17 years old, he flew all the way to Italy to compete in the World Youth Championships in Bressanone, representing the United States. Imagine being that young and already wearing your country's colors in a world competition! Of course, Ryan absolutely crushed it. He won gold in the shot put with a throw of 21.56 meters (which, by the way, was a championship record, no one had ever thrown that far in the history of the event) and grabbed a silver medal in the discus. Imagine the airport baggage claim after that trip—two giant shiny medals swinging from his neck, his luggage filled with competition gear, and all the airline staff asking him how it felt to be a world champion. The only thing left for him to do was keep growing, keep training, and break even more records.

By his senior year, the world already knew Ryan Crouser was special, but he wasn't satisfied yet. He was a Crouser after all, which meant greatness was expected. His final year in high school in 2011 was on top. After battling through a frustrating foot injury in his junior year, Ryan bounced back in an epic way. He went on to break the national high school indoor record in the shot put, launching a 5.44 kg (12 lb) shot put (that's about as heavy as a bowling ball) an insane 23.54 meters (nearly the length of two school buses!)—this was a "Can-you-believe-this-guy?" kind of record. This was the farthest any high school student in the entire United States had ever thrown indoors. Then, just to add some extra spice to his senior year, he set the national high school record for discus too, launching it an incredible 72.40 meters (which is almost the length of a football field!). Yup, it was a mic-drop moment. Breaking national records in both shot put and discus meant he was officially the best high school thrower in U.S. history up to that point.

But then came a pretty tough decision. You see, the Crousers were big-time University of Oregon fans. It was practically a family tradition. His dad, his uncles, his cousins—they all wore green and yellow. You could say the Crouser family practically bled Duck colors (the mascot of the University of Oregon is a duck). But when it came time to choose his college, Ryan didn't take the easy route or follow the crowd—he went his own way. He picked the University of Texas (a top school known for athletics), shaking up the family tradition. And while I'm sure there was some eyebrow-raising around the family dinner table, everyone knew Ryan was destined for greatness no matter where he went. It was less about where he studied and more about what he could accomplish once he got there.

Once Ryan arrived at the University of Texas, everything became about balance. No, I don't mean balancing on one leg—although, with all the box jumps and squats he was doing, he could probably do that, too. I'm talking about balancing between being a superstar athlete and also being a college student with all the challenges that come with it. You'd think it would be all shot puts and discus throws all day long, but Ryan actually started his college journey as an engineering student (studying complex math and science to design and build things). While throwing shot puts farther than anyone had ever seen, Ryan was also tackling some of the most complicated math and science problems you could think of. And let's be real, balancing engineering homework with training is like trying to juggle flaming swords while riding a unicycle.

But soon enough, Ryan realized that engineering wasn't going to give him the focus he needed for his athletic ambitions. It was like trying to throw a shot put with one hand tied behind his back. So, he made a smart move—he switched to economics (the study of how money and resources are used). And once he made that switch, he was able to hit his stride. College was a place where Ryan could figure out how to balance his crazy athletic talent with his academic goals. And he nailed it.

Even when he faced injuries, like the torn ligament in his hand during his freshman year or the foot injury that sidelined him during a critical meet, Ryan didn't let it slow him down. He bounced back every time, stronger, faster, and more determined than before. It was in college that he developed a work ethic so fierce that no setback could keep him down for long. In his sophomore year, Ryan won his first NCAA title (the best college athlete in the nation), throwing 21.09 meters at the 2013 Outdoor Championships. Throwing over 21 meters is a big deal in college shot put; it showed he was among the top throwers in the country. And let's not forget—this was after battling through injuries and the academic pressure of college life. He didn't even let the struggle of switching majors get in the way. When other students were stressing over midterms and finals, Ryan was breaking records, proving that you can be both brainy and brawny.

During his time at Texas, Ryan won four NCAA titles in shot put. Every title he claimed was like adding another jewel to a growing crown of achievements. In 2014, he grabbed another NCAA Indoor Championship title with a throw of 21.21 meters, then added a national title during the Outdoor Championships the same year. Each of these throws was not just good—they were among the best ever thrown by a college athlete. He was practically unstoppable, and despite dealing with an injury to his foot during his final throw of that outdoor season, Ryan still managed to walk away with his head held high and yet another title under his belt.

By the time he was a senior, Ryan was in his final stretch of college eligibility, and he wasn't about to waste it. At the 2016 Big 12 Indoor Championships, he pulled off something truly epic—a personal best of 21.73 meters in the shot put, matching the collegiate indoor record set by another shot put great, Ryan Whiting. Matching a collegiate record means he threw as far as anyone ever had in the history of college indoor competitions. It was the kind of moment where everyone in the arena just stopped and stared, jaws dropped, knowing they were witnessing something special.

But even with all the wins, all the titles, and all the records, Ryan was still focused on one thing: getting better every single day. For him, it wasn't just about breaking records; it was about constantly pushing the limits of what was possible. Every practice, every throw was a chance to be better than he was the day before. And that is how Ryan Crouser went from a giant in Boring, Oregon, to a champion at the University of Texas—still hungry, still throwing, and still dreaming of greater things to come.

After college, Ryan Crouser didn't step onto a yellow brick road leading to easy victories—he practically bulldozed his way through the most challenging and high-stakes competitions the world could throw at him. With his time at the University of Texas behind him, Ryan had set his sights on something far bigger, something that shimmered like a golden dream: the Olympics!

But here's the kicker—no one could have guessed just how far this giant from Boring, Oregon, would go.

The year was 2016. The world was buzzing with excitement for the Rio de Janeiro Summer Olympics, but for Ryan, it wasn't just another sporting event; it was the moment he had been preparing for his entire life. Sure, he'd already racked up NCAA titles and shattered records left and right, but now he was facing the biggest stage of them all—the Olympics. The stakes couldn't have been higher, and every single competitor there had their eye on that gold medal. He had his eyes on the shot put world. He was ready to show the entire planet what happens when you combine raw power, technique, and the heart of a champion.

So, there he was, standing in the Olympic ring (the circle from which athletes throw the shot put), all eyes on him. The stadium was packed, the pressure was mounting, and the world was watching. But Ryan was calm, cool, and collected—like a lion about to pounce, biding his time. When he finally stepped into the ring, he took a deep breath, steadied his feet, and then—BOOM!—he launched that shot put as if he were throwing a pebble across a pond. Except this was no pebble. This was a 16-pound ball of iron (that's as heavy as a full-grown beagle!) flying through the air at record speed.

The crowd gasped as the shot put sailed far, far beyond anything anyone expected. And when it finally landed—22.52 meters later (that's about 74 feet!)—Ryan Crouser had not just won gold; he had set a brand new Olympic record. Setting an Olympic record means he threw farther than anyone ever had in the entire history of the Olympic Games! Can you imagine? It was the first time an American man had won the event since 2004, and there Ryan was, standing at the top of the podium, with the whole world realizing they were witnessing the rise of a legend. "I was with Ryan in Rio when he won the gold medal," his coach later said, "and it was just the start of what was to come."

Ryan didn't stop there. He wasn't even close to done. Winning gold at Rio might have been enough for some athletes to retire with a grin and a shelf full of trophies, but Ryan was a Crouser. That meant he needed to push further, throw farther, and set more records. After Rio, he trained like a crazy to be the greatest shot putter in history. His eyes were set on every competition that mattered—World Championships (another big international competition), Diamond League events (a series of top-level track and field competitions), you name it.

Between 2016 and 2020, Ryan became a dominating force in the world of track and field. He grabbed national titles like they were candy at Halloween, competing against the best and consistently out-throwing them all. In 2020, when the world went into a shutdown due to the pandemic, most sports came to a screeching halt. But not for Ryan. He didn't sit around and wait for the world to reopen—he literally built his own shot put ring so he could keep training. This man was so determined to stay on top that he constructed his own throwing circle to make sure his throws never lost their distance. "To cope with the frustration of these shutdowns and maintain his competitive edge," Ryan said, he even dabbled in bass fishing—though throwing a 16-pound shot put and a fishing line couldn't be more different. But hey, it worked!

So when the Olympics finally rolled around again, this time in Tokyo in 2021. Tokyo was where the world saw Ryan Crouser 2.0, the evolved version. He walked into that Olympic ring and threw a monstrous 23.30 meters (over 76 feet!)—a distance that was so insane it set a brand new Olympic record! Breaking his own Olympic previous record from Rio, he threw even farther than himself before! Out of his six throws at Tokyo, three of them broke the previous Olympic record. I mean, the guy was obliterating the field, ahead of everyone else. Tokyo had been waiting for an epic showdown, and Ryan gave them a spectacle that people would be talking about for years. Two Olympic gold medals and two Olympic records in two separate games. At this point, there was no debate—Ryan was one of the greatest shot putters of all time.

But Ryan's story doesn't end there—because, of course, it doesn't, haha. After Tokyo, Ryan kept competing, and 2023 was the year when things really went off the charts. By now, Ryan wasn't just breaking Olympic records; he was smashing world records. In May of 2023, at the Los Angeles Grand Prix, he unleashed a jaw-dropping throw of 23.56 meters (that's nearly 77 feet!). Yup, you read that right. He beat his own previous world record and set a new outdoor world record. Setting a world record means he threw farther than anyone in the entire world ever had in history! How far can a shot put possibly fly? Well, Ryan was determined to find out.

And then came the 2024 Summer Olympics in Paris, the moment when Ryan had the chance to make history once again. This time, It was about becoming the first athlete ever to win three consecutive gold medals in shot put. No one had done it before. Ever. The shot put is an event that's brutal on the body, with every muscle, every bone, every tendon being pushed to the absolute limit. Three Olympics? That's an insane goal (since the Olympics happen every four years, that's over a decade of being the best).

Paris was a shot put showdown like no other, and once again, Ryan rose to the occasion. With the world holding its breath, he launched the shot put 22.90 meters (about 75 feet), winning his third Olympic gold. He was now a part of Olympic history, achieving something no shot putter had ever done before. Even Marcus Thompson of The Athletic had to admit: "What makes this one extra special is Crouser, at one point this year, thought his career was over." Yup, over. Just months before Paris, Ryan had battled injuries that made him question whether he could even compete again, let alone dominate the competition. But because he's Ryan Crouser, he bounced back stronger than ever, proving that not

And that's the thing about Ryan. Though he has plenty of records and medals, it was all about his drive, his refusal to settle for anything less than greatness. Every throw is a step toward being better than the day before. "I push myself because I want to be better," he once said, and he meant it. No matter how many records he breaks or how many gold medals he wins, Ryan never stops looking for that perfect throw. And if the past is any indication, we haven't seen the last of his epic throws yet. He's already redefined what's possible in the world of shot put—and something tells me he's not done breaking boundaries.

Scottie Scheffler

"The Greens Prodigy" ...Shattering Boundaries on the Golf Course

On a warm day in Ridgewood, New Jersey, 1996, Scottie Scheffler was born. His birth was like a tiny ripple in the ocean—a soft beginning to a story that would one day become a roaring wave. At the time, though, there was nothing but diapers, milk, and a lot of yawning. His parents, Diane and Scott, didn't know it, but this little boy would one day do extraordinary things—things that not even his wildest of wildest dreams could have predicted. At that time, Scottie was a regular kid dealing with the not-so-regular chaos that is life in the Scheffler household.

Scottie had three sisters, Callie, Molly, and Sara. And if you're thinking, "What's it like growing up with three sisters?" Well, I'll tell you. Imagine you're the only boy in the house, and every day is like being trapped in a never-ending episode of a sitcom. Callie is yelling about a missing hairbrush, Sara's arguing over who stole the last cookie, and Molly is... well, Molly's just there to add some dramatic flair to the whole situation. "The noise level was always off the charts," Scottie would say years later, shaking his head with a chuckle. But despite the constant, buzzing energy, there was an undeniable love in that house—a love that tied them all together, even when they wanted to pull each other's hair out.

Scottie's dad, Scott Scheffler, stayed home with the kids. Staying at home with four children is a bit like being the captain of a pirate ship. You've got to keep them from throwing each other overboard while also keeping everyone from tearing the sails to shreds. His mom, Diane, was a superhero in her own right, working in New York City as a business manager (someone who helps run a company) at a law firm (a company where lawyers work) called Skadden. Later, she became the chief operating officer (the top person in charge of daily operations) at another law firm in Dallas. She wasn't around during the day because she was busy taking on the world in the city that never sleeps, but when she was home, she brought the kind of energy that could fuel a rocket ship.

And even though Scottie's parents came from wildly different places—his dad growing up in Englewood Cliffs, New Jersey, and his mom in Park Ridge, where she was friends with the legendary James Gandolfini, aka Tony Soprano (yes, that Tony Soprano famous TV character)—they both agreed on one thing: their kids came first. They weren't ordinary parents; they were the type of parents who shoveled snow off a driving range, where golfers practice hitting balls, in the middle of winter so their son could practice his swing. They were the type of parents who would pack up their entire life and move to Dallas, Texas, when Scottie was six years old, all in the name of giving him and his sisters a safer and better life after a tragic event that happened in New York in 2001. And this was Dallas, not New Jersey. A whole new world for young Scottie.

Now, when you're a small kid (Scottie was "barely 5 feet" entering high school), moving can feel like the end of the universe. But for Scottie, it turned out to be the beginning of something magical. In Dallas, his parents borrowed $50,000—a huge, ginormous, totally epic sum of money that could've bought, like, a zillion video games—to join the Royal Oaks Country Club, a fancy golf club where members can play and practice. This place was like stepping into the halls of a legendary castle for golfers. The kind of castle where future champions were made, where dreams were molded out of long hours on the putting green (the area where golfers practice putting the ball into the hole), and where every blade of grass seemed to whisper, "You're going to be great, kid."

But before that could happen, Scottie had to learn the ropes. And for a kid who, at age three, had been given a plastic set of golf clubs by his parents, this was like living out a fairy tale. His father remembered how Scottie, even as a little guy, practiced by hitting ping-pong balls in their house. And not just normal straight shots, mind you. This kid was curving them, making them fly through doorways and around corners like a magician in training. It was like he was preparing for the world of golf before he even knew what golf really was. And so, with that same determination, little Scottie would drag his dad out to the 9W Driving Range near the Hudson River back in New Jersey, begging to hit real golf balls. No snowstorm or chilly weather could stop him—Scottie was relentless. "When you're shoveling snow to practice golf, you know you're serious," Scottie would later laugh.

So there he was, in Dallas, at Royal Oaks, this kid with fire in his heart and a club in his hand. His coach, Randy Smith, who had guided pros like Justin Leonard, took him under his wing and started mentoring him. It was like having Yoda as your coach—if Yoda could swing a golf club, that is. Scottie wasn't just surrounded by ordinary people either. He had a front-row seat to watch pros like Leonard, Ryan Palmer, and Harrison Frazar at work. By the time Scottie was nine years old, he was challenging these guys to chipping (short shots to get the ball onto the green) and putting contests! Nine years old and already going head-to-head with pros? Who does that? Well, apparently Scottie Scheffler does.

And so, the legend began to grow. Scottie, now towering at over 6 feet tall thanks to a major growth spurt, started dominating the Northern Texas PGA junior circuit, a series of golf tournaments for young players in Northern Texas, racking up wins like it was some sort of video game and he had unlocked all the cheat codes. Between 2004 and 2010, he won an unbelievable 90 out of the 136 tournaments he entered. Let that sink; 90 wins. Imagine winning so many trophies that your room would probably look more like a mini-museum. Even then, Scottie was becoming known for his fierce competitive spirit, something his dad said was definitely inherited. "A lot of my personality probably comes from my dad. My dad is fiercely competitive like I am," Scottie said, like this was some kind of family superpower.

Through all this, Scottie was becoming a better golfer and also a better person. His parents never pushed him to be the next big thing. They cared more about who he was as a person than what he did on the course. "My parents made a lot of sacrifices to put me in a position where I'm able to do this for a living, and they made a lot of sacrifices when I was a kid," Scottie would say, reflecting on all the love and effort they put into his upbringing.

In those days, life wasn't about the big stuff, though. It wasn't about the Masters (a famous golf tournament) or PGA championships; another major golf tournament. It was about family, snow-covered driving ranges, and the small wins that would one day turn into huge victories. Scottie might've been growing taller and stronger by the minute, but inside, he was still just a kid from Dallas who loved his sisters, listened to his dad's advice, and sometimes thought his mom's job was cooler than his friends' moms because of her connection to Tony Soprano. Scottie was still Scottie—only now, the wind had begun to blow, and soon enough, it would carry him to places far beyond anyone's imaginations.

GOLF IS A SPORT WHERE YOU TRY TO HIT A SMALL BALL INTO A HOLE USING AS FEW HITS AS POSSIBLE. EACH HIT IS CALLED A "STROKE." A FULL GAME HAS 18 HOLES, AND EACH HOLE IS DIFFERENT. SOME ARE LONG, SOME ARE SHORT, AND THERE ARE OBSTACLES LIKE SAND OR WATER TO MAKE IT TRICKIER. EACH HOLE HAS A NUMBER CALLED "PAR," WHICH TELLS YOU HOW MANY HITS (STROKES) A GOOD PLAYER SHOULD TAKE TO GET THE BALL INTO THE HOLE. FOR EXAMPLE, IF THE PAR IS 4, IT MEANS A GOOD PLAYER SHOULD BE ABLE TO FINISH THE HOLE IN 4 HITS. IF YOU DO IT IN FEWER STROKES, LIKE 3, THAT'S CALLED "UNDER PAR" AND IS GREAT! IF IT TAKES YOU MORE STROKES, LIKE 5, THAT'S CALLED "OVER PAR," AND THAT'S NOT AS GOOD. GOLFERS USE DIFFERENT TOOLS CALLED "CLUBS" TO HIT THE BALL. WHEN THEY NEED TO HIT THE BALL REALLY FAR, THEY USE A CLUB CALLED A "DRIVER." WHEN THEY'RE CLOSE TO THE HOLE, THEY USE A "PUTTER" TO GENTLY ROLL THE BALL IN. THE PLAYER'S SCORE IS THE TOTAL NUMBER OF STROKES THEY TAKE FOR ALL 18 HOLES. THE FEWER STROKES YOU TAKE, THE BETTER YOUR SCORE! AT THE END, THE PLAYER WITH THE LOWEST SCORE (THE FEWEST STROKES) WINS.

As the wind carried Scottie into his high school years, something remarkable began to happen. Remember that kid who was "barely 5 feet" tall? Well, somewhere between dodging basketballs and perfecting his swing, Scottie Scheffler hit a growth spurt so gigantic that it felt like one day he was putting balls around his backyard, and the next day, he was towering over the competition at over six feet tall. It was like watching a beanstalk grow overnight, except this beanstalk had a wicked golf swing and a killer jump shot.

At Highland Park High School, Scottie wasn't just any regular kid trying to make it through math class without falling asleep. No, he was the kid. The kid everyone wanted to know. Not because he was showing off—because showing off was never Scottie's style—but because no matter what sport he tried, he was great at it. Basketball, football, baseball, even lacrosse—he did it all like he was born for it. But there was something about golf that pulled him in like a magnet, something about the quiet focus, the lone battle of you versus the ball, that felt like it was meant for him.

And Scottie was unstoppable at golf. He rolled through the Northern Texas PGA junior circuit like a freight train made of sunshine and winning smiles, racking up 90 wins and leaving everyone else wondering how this kid seemed to have a magic wand hidden in his golf bag. But even as he balanced school, sports, and the wild rollercoaster of teenage life, Scottie remained humble. He never acted like he was better than anyone else; he was still the same kid who played chipping contests with pros at Royal Oaks and got nervous before big tournaments.

By the time Scottie entered high school, people were already whispering his name in the halls. Not because of some silly rumor or because he had done anything wrong (he never did, this is Scottie we're talking about), but because he was about to pull off something that hadn't been done since another Texas golf legend, Jordan Spieth. Scottie won the individual state golf title (the championship for the best high school golfer in the state) not once, not twice, but three times in a row between 2012 and 2014. Three straight years of Scottie Scheffler standing at the top of the mountain with a shiny trophy in his hand, grinning that big ol' grin of his.

Winning those state titles wasn't easy, of course. The pressure was there, lurking like a shadow over every swing, but Scottie always found a way to keep calm. His dad, Scott, who had been his first caddie (the person who carries a golfer's clubs and gives advice) and biggest fan, was often by his side. He'd seen his son grow from that tiny kid hitting ping-pong balls in the house to this towering golfer with a heart of gold and a swing so smooth it made people stop in their tracks. "A lot of my personality probably comes from my dad," Scottie would say, crediting the fierce competitiveness that drove him forward to his father. And did that competitiveness come in handy.

You'd think that with all those victories and trophies piling up, Scottie might start getting a little big-headed. But that wasn't him. Scottie was the kid who would win a tournament and then go home to his sisters and argue over whose turn it was to pick the next movie for family movie night. He'd help out around the house, make sure his homework was done, and probably sneak in a game of basketball in the driveway before bedtime. That's just how he rolled.

And while golf was clearly becoming his thing, Scottie wasn't ready to give up basketball. He loved shooting hoops, and even though he was short until his growth spurt, he could sink three-pointers like they were layups. In fact, during one memorable practice, he made 30 consecutive three-pointers in a row. "I still love basketball," Scottie said later. "It's my favorite sport to watch on TV." It's not hard to imagine him standing in front of the television, eyes glued to an NBA game, fingers itching for a basketball, just like how his mind must've sometimes wandered toward the golf course, thinking of his next swing.

But as high school went on, Scottie had to make a choice: basketball or golf? He couldn't do both forever, not at the level he wanted to. It was like choosing between two best friends who both wanted to hang out with him at the same time. Eventually, though, golf won out. It was his passion, the one sport he couldn't get out of his head. "My whole life, I knew how much I loved golf," he once said. "It was the one sport I always wanted to be playing, regardless of the season."

And so, Scottie Scheffler, now standing tall at over six feet, with hands that seemed to have been carved specifically for gripping golf clubs, threw himself into the game. He was relentless. Every practice, every swing, every single putt—he did it with the focus of someone who knew exactly what he wanted and was willing to work for it. And it didn't take long before the University of Texas came knocking on his door. They weren't about to let a talent like Scottie slip away.

Now, the University of Texas isn't just some random school with a golf team. It's the University of Texas, a powerhouse in college sports, and Scottie was about to join a legendary program. This was the same school that had produced other golf greats, like Ben Crenshaw and Jordan Spieth. It was a place where champions were made, and Scottie was about to carve his name into that history. In 2014, Scottie arrived at the University of Texas as a freshman, and did he make an impression. He did dominate the college life, winning his first individual collegiate title (a championship for college golfers) at the Western Intercollegiate in April 2015. Two weeks later, he did it again, claiming victory at the Big 12 Individual Championship (a major college golf tournament in their athletic conference) at Southern Hills Country Club. You could almost hear the gasps from his opponents—who was this freshman who seemed to have an extra gear that no one else could find?

And then, there was the award. Oh, yes, the award. Scottie was named the 2015 "Phil Mickelson Freshman of the Year," which is basically like being handed a golden crown and told, "Congrats, you're officially one of the best young golfers in the country." But of course, Scottie didn't let it go to his head. He just smiled, thanked his teammates, and went back to work.

But even for someone like Scottie, who seemed to win at everything he did, life wasn't always a straight shot down the fairway. During his sophomore season, Scottie faced a serious challenge: back injuries. Now, anyone who's played golf—or even tried to swing a club once—knows how important your back is to your game. And for a young golfer like Scottie, who was still adapting to his new, taller body, back pain was a major roadblock. His coach, John Fields, said Scottie was going through a massive transformation. "He's gone from 5-foot-2, 100 pounds in eighth grade to almost 6-foot-4, 200 pounds just six years later," Fields explained. That's like watching someone grow from a mouse into a mountain lion almost overnight! But Scottie, ever the fighter, didn't let the pain stop him. Sure, he struggled that season, recording only one top-10 finish (placing among the top ten players in a tournament), but he didn't let it drag him down. He focused on getting better—he knew this was just a bump in the road, and soon enough, he'd be back to his winning ways.

By the time 2016 rolled around, Scottie had shaken off those back issues and was back on the rise. That summer, he qualified for the U.S. Open (one of the four major tournaments in professional golf), a huge deal for any golfer, let alone a college kid. Not only did he qualify, but he shot an impressive first-round 69 (completing the round in 69 strokes, which is three strokes under par—a very good score), grabbing the overnight lead. Can you imagine? A college sophomore leading the U.S. Open, one of the biggest tournaments in the world, like it was just a casual round of golf on a Saturday morning? Of course, things didn't go perfectly—he shot a 78 in the second round and missed the cut (didn't qualify to continue playing in the final rounds) by one stroke—but that first day was a glimpse into Scottie's potential. It was like seeing a lightning bolt flash across the sky and knowing a storm of talent was about to hit.

And Scottie didn't stop there. In 2017, he again qualified for the U.S. Open, and this time, he didn't miss the cut. He and another up-and-coming golfer, Cameron Champ, were the only amateurs (non-professional golfers) to make it through to the weekend. Scottie finished as the low amateur (the amateur with the best score), shooting 1-under-par (completing the course one stroke under par) and beating Champ by a single stroke. It was another feather in his cap, another sign that Scottie Scheffler wasn't just a good golfer—he was special.

But even as Scottie's golf career was skyrocketing, he remained grounded. He was still the kid from Dallas who loved his family, went to church, and kept his friends close. He became a member of the Texas Cowboys, a service-based student organization, during his time at the University of Texas. The Cowboys are known for their commitment to community service and tradition, and Scottie fit right in. It wasn't all about golf for him—it was about being a good person, someone who gave back to the community and lived with purpose.

By the time Scottie graduated from the University of Texas in 2018 with a bachelor's degree in finance, he had already made a name for himself as one of the top amateur golfers in the country. He had competed in two U.S. Opens, won multiple college tournaments, and represented the United States at the 2017 Walker Cup (a prestigious team competition between amateur golfers from the U.S. and Great Britain & Ireland), where he helped lead his team to a dominating victory.

But more than anything, Scottie had proven that no matter how tall he grew, how far he hit the ball, or how many trophies he won, he would always be the same grounded, humble kid who loved his family, his faith, and, of course, a good round of golf. Little did he know, the world of professional golf was waiting for him, and the wind that had carried him so far was about to blow him into a new and exciting chapter of his life.

Scottie Scheffler graduated from the University of Texas in 2018 with a degree in finance, but his future wasn't going to involve cubicles, spreadsheets, and awkward watercooler conversations. Scottie was destined for different things. Armed with his degree, a golf bag full of clubs, and the kind of self-belief you could bottle and sell as confidence juice, he became a professional golfer. It was time for Scottie to enter the wild world of professional golf, a place where dreams could either soar higher than an eagle (a score of two strokes under par on a hole) or crash harder than a triple bogey (three strokes over par). And soar, Scottie did.

But before he became a superstar, there were some bumps on the road. Professional golf is like entering a jungle full of seasoned lions, and Scottie had to prove that his roar was just as fierce. He kicked things off on the Korn Ferry Tour (a series of tournaments where golfers compete to earn a spot on the PGA Tour) in 2019, and of course, it didn't take long for Scottie to start winning. In May 2019, at the Evans Scholars Invitational, he unleashed a mind-blowing, bogey-free (no holes scored over par) 9-under 63 (completing the round in 63 strokes, which is nine under par) to force a playoff (an extra round to break a tie)—and then coolly birdied (scored one stroke under par) the second extra hole to win. One win down, countless more to go. He finished the entire tournament with a final score of 17-under par, meaning he completed the whole tournament with 17 strokes fewer than what was expected for the course.

By August 2019, Scottie had added another victory to his collection at the Nationwide Children's Hospital Championship, winning by two shots. These wins catapulted him to the top of the Korn Ferry Tour standings, earning him not only a PGA Tour card (his ticket to compete in the main professional golf tour in the U.S.) but the prestigious Korn Ferry Tour Player of the Year title. At this point, it was clear that Scottie was no ordinary rookie. He was a fireball of talent that couldn't be contained. And now, with a PGA Tour card in hand, he was ready to take on the biggest stage in golf.

In 2020, Scottie was officially a PGA Tour rookie, and what a rookie season it was. He finished tied for fourth at the PGA Championship (one of the four major championships in professional golf), which was a jaw-dropping result for a guy in his first year. But that wasn't even the craziest part. In August of that year, at The Northern Trust, Scottie shot a blistering 12-under 59 (completing the round in 59 strokes, which is exceptionally rare) in the second round—a score so low it seemed like it should come with a flashing neon sign and a fireworks display. This made him the 12th player in PGA Tour history to break 60, and suddenly, everyone knew his name. Scottie Scheffler wasn't just another guy on the tour. He was something special, like a rare gem unearthed on a cloudy day. And to top it off, he was named PGA Tour Rookie of the Year for the 2019-2020 season. Pretty impressive for a guy who was still driving his old college car—a Chevy Suburban with over 175,000 miles on it.

This was only the beginning. With Bubba Watson's former caddie, Ted Scott, by his side, Scottie began 2022 on an absolute tear. In February, he grabbed his first PGA Tour win at the WM Phoenix Open, taking down Patrick Cantlay in a playoff (an extra session to determine the winner) like it was no big deal. Three weeks later, he added another victory at the Arnold Palmer Invitational. Three weeks after that, he won the WGC-Dell Technologies Match Play. And with that, Scottie soared to world number one in the Official World Golf Ranking (he was ranked as the best golfer in the world). At 25 years old, he was the sixth-youngest player to ever claim the top spot since the rankings began in 1986. Boom.

But the biggest prize of all was waiting for him in April 2022: the Masters Tournament. The hallowed grounds of Augusta National have witnessed plenty of champions, but Scottie made his own special mark. That week, he played like a man possessed, dominating the field and winning his first major by three strokes over Rory McIlroy. The green jacket was his, a symbol of all his hard work and relentless dedication. (In the Masters Tournament, the winner is awarded a green jacket as a sign of honor.) "It's hard to put into words how special this is," Scottie said afterward, looking almost bewildered at his own success. "It's been a long week, a grind of a week. To be sitting here wearing this jacket… it's extremely special."

Over the next two years, he became a constant force on the PGA Tour, a player so good that even his fellow competitors shook their heads in awe. In 2023, he successfully defended his WM Phoenix Open title (won the same tournament two years in a row) and added a new feather to his cap with a five-stroke victory at The Players Championship, also known as golf's "fifth major" (a very prestigious tournament). And, of course, he didn't stop there—because Scottie Scheffler doesn't know how to stop. He was relentless, laser-focused, and always pushing forward.

Came 2024, a year that might as well have been called "The Year of Scottie." It was like he was on a never-ending victory tour, winning one tournament after another, as if the universe itself had decided to cheer him on. He kicked off the year with his second Masters victory, this time by four strokes, joining an elite club of two-time champions at Augusta. Then he won the Arnold Palmer Invitational again, claimed back-to-back victories at The Players Championship, and added more trophies at the RBC Heritage, the Memorial Tournament, and the Travelers Championship. By the time June rolled around, Scottie had already claimed six wins in 10 starts—an absolutely ridiculous pace that hadn't been seen since the days of Tiger Woods (one of the greatest golfers ever) in the early 2000s. But there was one more prize waiting for Scottie in 2024: the Summer Olympics in Paris.

Now, golf in the Olympics might not have the same centuries-old prestige as the Masters or the Open Championship (also known as the British Open, one of the four major championships in golf), but to Scottie, representing his country on the global stage was an incredible honor. He arrived in Paris as the world's number one golfer, the heavy favorite to win gold. But the pressure didn't faze him. If there's one thing we know about Scottie Scheffler, it's that he thrives under pressure. He loves the challenge, the grind, the thrill of competition.

At Le Golf National, where the event was held, Scottie faced a tough field that included the best golfers from around the world. After three rounds, he found himself six strokes behind the leader, but this was Scottie Scheffler—he didn't panic. On the final day, with the wind blowing and the tension high, Scottie shot a dazzling 62 (completing the round in 62 strokes, a very good score), tying the course record. Six birdies (scores of one stroke under par on a hole) on the back nine (the last nine holes of an 18-hole course) lifted him to a one-stroke victory over England's Tommy Fleetwood. It was a comeback for the ages, and when Scottie tapped in his final putt, he raised his arms in triumph. The gold medal was his, another symbol of excellence to add to his growing collection.

The Olympics were a little different from the other tournaments he'd won, though. It wasn't just about Scottie. It was about representing his country, standing on that podium with the American flag flying high, the national anthem playing in the background. For Scottie, it was a moment that transcended golf. "Winning gold for my country is something I'll never forget," he said, still holding the medal in his hands like he couldn't quite believe it was real. "It's been an amazing journey, and I'm just thankful for the opportunity to be here."

As the 2024 season continued. He entered the Tour Championship, the final event of the PGA Tour season, as the leader in the FedEx Cup standings (the season-long points competition) for the third year in a row. This time, he wasn't going to let it slip away. With a dominant performance at East Lake Golf Club, Scottie finished 30-under-par (completing the tournament with a total score 30 strokes under par) and claimed the FedEx Cup title. This win cemented his legacy as one of the greatest golfers of his generation.

By the end of the 2024 season, Scottie had earned millions in on-course earnings, shattering records and making it clear that he was a phenomenon. His blend of talent, humility, and unwavering faith made him a fan favorite and an inspiration to golfers everywhere. His success was built not just on his incredible skill but on his grounded approach to life, his faith, and his family. He and his wife, Meredith, welcomed their first child, Bennett, in May 2024, and Scottie made it clear that while he loved competing, his family always came first. "I definitely will enjoy the birth of my first child, and my priorities will change very soon, so golf will be fourth in line," Scottie said with a smile. "But I still love competing. I don't plan on taking my eye off the ball anytime soon."

And with that, Scottie Scheffler—the kid who once hit ping-pong balls through doorways, the college star who fought through back injuries, the PGA Tour phenom who couldn't stop winning—had become something more. He was an Olympic champion, a multiple major winner, and a golfer for the ages. But more than that, he was a good person, a devoted husband and father, and someone who believed in treating people with kindness and living his life with purpose.

Amazing Facts, Records, and Moments

The Evolution of Olympic Glory

From Ancient Greece Until Now!

The Birth of the Games: Ancient Olympics and the Origins of Modern Sport

Once Upon a Time in Ancient Greece:

Over 2,700 years ago, in 776 BCE (that's "Before Common Era," a way we count years long ago), the very first Olympic Games were held in Olympia—a special place with temples and arenas dedicated to Zeus, the king of the gods in Greek mythology (the stories and legends of ancient Greece). Back then, people believed in many gods who they thought controlled everything in the world, like the weather and the seas.

Athletes from all over Greece traveled (on foot or by ship—no cars, trains, or planes back then!) to compete and show off their skills. These Games happened every four years, and this period was called an Olympiad—a fancy Greek way of counting four years between Games. Fun fact: athletes competed wearing no clothes at all! In those times, competing naked was normal and seen as a tribute to the gods, celebrating the human body's beauty and strength. The Olympics weren't just about competitions; they were huge festivals filled with feasts, music, and cheering crowds. It was like the biggest party in ancient Greece!

Athletes of Ancient Times:

In the ancient Olympics, only freeborn Greek men (men who were born free citizens, not slaves) could compete—sorry, no girls or slaves allowed! Back then, society was very different, and women weren't allowed to participate in or even watch the Games. These athletes trained super hard to showcase their strength and skill. Winning wasn't just about bragging rights (being able to boast); victors were treated like superheroes! Instead of gold medals, they received olive wreaths made from sacred trees (crowns made from special olive branches). Imagine getting crowned with leaves and everyone cheering your name! Back home, they might get free meals for life, front-row seats at events, and even statues built in their honor. Being an Olympic champion was a really big deal!

Honoring the King of the Gods:

The Olympics were like a giant birthday party for Zeus! Sports were a way to honor him, and winning athletes were thought to have his special favor. The olive wreaths weren't just cool headgear—they symbolized peace, victory, and a connection to the divine (the gods). Picture coming home to a hero's welcome because the king of the gods gave you a thumbs-up!

Events Fit for Legends:

The Games started with a simple footrace but soon grew to include wrestling, boxing, long jump, javelin throw, discus throw, and chariot racing (imagine zooming around in a cart pulled by horses!). There was also the pentathlon—a super challenge combining five events: running, long jump, discus throw, javelin throw, and wrestling. One of the wildest events was the pankration, a mix of boxing and wrestling with almost no rules (no biting or eye-gouging—that's it! Eye-gouging means poking someone's eyes). Athletes competed without helmets or pads—just pure guts and glory! Safety gear and protective equipment weren't invented yet, so competitions were pretty rough.

The End of an Era:

The ancient Olympics ran for nearly 1,200 years! But in 393 AD, Roman Emperor Theodosius I, who wanted everyone to follow Christianity (believing in one God instead of many), banned all pagan festivals (celebrations honoring many gods)—including the Olympics that honored gods like Zeus. The Games stopped, and Olympia fell into ruins, buried over time until archaeologists (scientists who study ancient places) rediscovered it in the 1800s. The ancient Olympic spirit went into a long sleep, waiting to be awakened centuries later!

Olympic Symbols: The Meaning and Evolution of the Rings, Torch, and Motto

The Five Rings of Unity:

In 1913, Baron Pierre de Coubertin—the Frenchman who revived (brought back to life) the modern Olympics—designed the iconic Olympic rings. These five interlocking rings represent the five continents involved in the Games: Africa, the Americas, Asia, Europe, and Oceania (that's places like Australia and the Pacific Islands). The rings are linked to show how the Olympics bring the whole world together like one big team! The symbol first appeared at the 1920 Antwerp Games and has been inspiring unity ever since.

Colors That Connect the World:

Why these ring colors? Blue, yellow, black, green, and red on a white background were chosen because every country's flag in the world includes at least one of these colors! It's like a rainbow that wraps around the globe, saying, "We're all part of the Olympic family!" So, when you see the rings, you're seeing a piece of every nation on Earth.

The Journey of the Flame:

In ancient times, a sacred fire burned throughout the Olympics. Inspired by this, the Olympic flame was brought back in 1928. Then, in 1936, the torch relay was introduced: the flame is lit at Olympia in Greece and carried all the way to the host city (the city where the Olympics are held). Runners, boats, planes, camels, and even divers have helped transport it—once, it even went into space! The flame represents peace, hope, and the passing of traditions from one generation to the next. It's like a glowing handshake from the past to the future!

A Motto to Inspire:

The Olympic motto "Citius, Altius, Fortius" is Latin (an ancient language from Rome) for "Faster, Higher, Stronger." Proposed by de Coubertin in 1894, he got the idea from his friend Father Henri Didon, who used it to encourage his students. The motto inspires athletes to push their limits and reach for the stars (literally, in pole vaulting!). In 2021, the word "Together" was added, making it "Faster, Higher, Stronger—Together," to highlight the power of teamwork. It's like saying, "Let's all be awesome—together!"

Symbols That Speak Volumes:

The rings, the flame, the motto—they're more than just cool designs. They're powerful messages about going beyond our limits, making friends across the globe, and uniting the world through sports. They remind us that the Olympics aren't just about winning medals; they're about celebrating what humans can achieve when we come together. It's like a worldwide high-five!

Key Milestones: Significant Changes in the Olympic Format

Winter Games Take the Stage:

Before 1924, some chilly sports sneaked into the Summer Olympics, but athletes wanted their own winter wonderland! So, the first official Winter Olympics were held in 1924 in Chamonix, France, featuring skiing, ice hockey, figure skating, and more. Now, every four years, athletes zoom down slopes and glide on ice in the Winter Games. It's like the Olympics put on a warm coat and mittens to play in the snow!

Women Join the Competition:

In the 1900 Paris Olympics, women were allowed to compete for the first time—hooray! Out of nearly 1,000 athletes, 22 were women. Hélène de Pourtalès from Switzerland became the first female Olympic champion in sailing. Back then, women didn't have the same rights as men and were often excluded from sports and many other activities. Fast forward, and now women compete in every sport. By the 2012 London Games, every country included female athletes. Girls rock the Games just as much as boys, inspiring the world with their amazing talents!

Paralympics: Celebrating All Abilities

In 1960, the first Paralympic Games were held in Rome, thanks to Dr. Ludwig Guttmann, who wanted to help injured soldiers from World War II (a huge war from 1939 to 1945 involving many countries) through sports. Back then, people with disabilities often didn't have opportunities to participate in sports or many public events. Starting with 400 athletes from 23 countries, the Paralympics have grown into a huge event held right after the Olympics, using the same stadiums! These Games show that no matter the challenges, athletes can achieve incredible things. It's proof that sports truly are for everyone!

Youth Olympics: The Next Generation:

The Youth Olympic Games kicked off in 2010, giving athletes aged 14 to 18 their own international stage. But it's not just about winning medals; the Games mix sports with cultural exchanges (sharing traditions and learning about other countries) and educational programs. Think of it as a global sports festival where young athletes compete, make friends from around the world, and learn cool stuff. It's the ultimate sports camp!

Adding New and Exciting Sports:

The Olympics like to keep things fresh by adding new sports! In Tokyo 2020 (held in 2021 due to a delay from the COVID-19 pandemic—a time when a virus caused many events to be postponed), skateboarding, surfing, karate, and sport climbing made their Olympic debut, along with the return of baseball and softball. These sports bring youthful energy and reflect what people love today. Imagine grabbing a gold medal for shredding on a skateboard, hanging ten on a surfboard (riding a wave), or scaling a wall like Spider-Man!

Olympics and the World: The Role of the Games in Global Politics, Social Change, and Unity

A Time for Peace:

Guess what? In ancient Greece, they paused all wars so athletes and spectators could travel safely to the Olympics. This peace agreement was called the Olympic Truce. Imagine warriors putting down their swords and shields to watch some sports! Today, the Olympic Truce inspires efforts to promote peace during the Games. While it's not always perfect, it shows how the Olympics aim to unite the world—even if it's just for a little while.

Cold War Competitions:

From the 1950s to the 1980s, the USA and the Soviet Union (a big country that included Russia and other nations) were rivals in what's called the Cold War (a period of tension and competition without actual fighting). Back then, the world was divided between countries with different ideas about government and how people should live. They didn't fight battles but competed fiercely in the Olympics! Winning medals became a way to prove whose country was better. It turned the Games into a high-stakes showdown. Remember the "Miracle on Ice" in 1980 when the US hockey team beat the Soviet team? It was more than just a game—it was a legendary moment where underdogs (the team not expected to win) triumphed!

Boycotts and Their Impact:

In 1980, the USA and over 60 other countries decided not to go to the Moscow Olympics to protest (show disapproval of) the Soviet Union's actions in Afghanistan. Then, in

1984, the Soviet Union and its friends skipped the Los Angeles Games in return. These boycotts (when countries refuse to participate) meant many athletes missed their big chance to shine after years of training. It shows how politics (the way countries make decisions) can sometimes get in the way of sports and athletes' dreams—a real bummer!

Moments of Unity and Hope:

At the 2000 Sydney Olympics, athletes from North and South Korea (two countries that are usually not on friendly terms due to political differences) marched together under one flag—a powerful symbol of hope and unity! There are many such moments where the Olympics bring people together, even from countries that don't always get along. It's like sports magic, showing that when it comes to the Games, we're all part of one big team.

Fun Finale: Fascinating Olympic Tidbits

The Evolution of Medals:

Back in the first modern Olympics in 1896, winners got silver medals and olive branches—no gold medals yet! Gold medals made their debut in 1904. But guess what? Today's "gold" medals are mostly silver with a tiny layer of gold. A solid gold medal would be super heavy and cost a fortune! So, when athletes bite their medals for photos, they're mostly tasting silver.

Youngest and Oldest Olympians:

Imagine competing in the Olympics at age 10! That's what Dimitrios Loundras did in 1896 in gymnastics, making him the youngest Olympian ever. On the flip side, Oscar Swahn from Sweden won a silver medal in shooting at age 72 in 1920! He also snagged gold medals when he was 64 and 68. These amazing athletes prove that in the Olympics, age is just a number. Whether you're a kid or a grandparent, you can go for the gold!

The Marathon's Royal Distance:

Did you know the marathon wasn't always 26.2 miles? Before 1908, marathon distances varied. But during the London Olympics that year, the race started at Windsor Castle (so the royal kids could watch the start!) and finished in front of King Edward VII's royal box (the special seating area for the king and queen) at the stadium—a distance of 26 miles and 385 yards. This royal tweak became the standard distance for marathons everywhere—a king-sized decision that stuck!

Olympic Torch's Space Adventure:

The Olympic torch has been around the world—and even out of this world! In 2013, for the Sochi Winter Games, the torch hitched a ride on a Russian Soyuz spacecraft and went on a spacewalk outside the International Space Station (a giant station orbiting Earth where astronauts live and work together—though the flame wasn't lit for safety reasons). The torch has also been underwater and to the top of Mount Everest. Talk about taking the Olympic spirit to new heights and depths!

From ancient athletes running in honor of Zeus to modern Olympians taking the torch to space, the Olympics have transformed into a worldwide celebration of what humans can achieve. Over time, the Games have added cool new sports, welcomed athletes of all abilities and genders, and promoted peace and friendship. They inspire us to push our limits and unite, proving that through sports, we really can make the world a better, more exciting place!

Weird, Wild, and Wacky Olympic Moments

The Games' Funniest and Most Unusual Highlights

Oddball Sports: From Tug of War to Croquet—The Weirdest Sports Ever Played at the Olympics

Tug of War at the Olympics?

Believe it or not, from 1900 to 1920, Tug of War was an official Olympic sport! Teams of strong athletes pulled on opposite ends of a rope, trying to drag the other team across a line. It was like the ultimate playground game on the world's biggest stage. Imagine winning a gold medal for pulling a rope really hard! Back then, the Olympics included many sports that seem unusual today because they wanted to showcase a wide variety of physical skills.

Live Pigeon Shooting: A Feathered Fiasco

In the 1900 Paris Olympics, there was an event called Live Pigeon Shooting. Yes, participants aimed at real birds! Over 300 pigeons were released, and the goal was to shoot as many as possible. It was the only time this event was held, and afterward, they decided to switch to clay targets (fake birds made of clay). Today, we protect animals, so this event seems really strange! At that time, attitudes toward animals were different, and conservation wasn't a big concern yet.

Plunge for Distance: Dive and Glide

At the 1904 St. Louis Olympics, athletes competed in Plunge for Distance. They would dive into a pool and see how far they could glide underwater without moving their arms or legs. It was like being a human torpedo! The winner managed to glide over 62 feet (about 19 meters) before surfacing. Swimming techniques were still developing back then, and people were fascinated by underwater feats.

Solo Synchronized Swimming: Wait, What?

In the 1984, 1988, and 1992 Olympics, there was an event called Solo Synchronized Swimming. But how do you synchronize with yourself? The swimmers performed routines in the water to music, showcasing grace and artistry. Even though it sounds funny, it required a lot of skill and imagination. "Synchronized" here means matching movements perfectly with the music's rhythm.

Croquet and Roque: Lawn Games Gone Olympic

The 1900 Paris Olympics also featured Croquet, a lawn game where players hit balls through hoops using mallets. Only French players participated, and only one spectator watched the event! In 1904, the USA introduced Roque, a version of croquet played on a hard surface. These sports didn't catch on and were soon dropped. Including these games shows how the Olympics once experimented with different sports that were popular locally.

Mascot Madness: The Funniest and Most Unusual Olympic Mascots Throughout History

Schuss: The Skiing Teardrop

The first unofficial Olympic mascot was Schuss at the 1968 Grenoble Winter Olympics. Schuss was a little man on skis shaped like a teardrop with a big smile. He looked like a cartoon character zooming down the slopes! Mascots were introduced to make the Games more fun and engaging, especially for kids.

Wenlock and Mandeville: The One-Eyed Wonders

For the 2012 London Olympics, the mascots were Wenlock and Mandeville, two shiny, one-eyed creatures made from droplets of steel. They had lights on their heads and were said to be formed from the last girder (a big steel beam) used to build the Olympic Stadium. Some thought they looked like friendly aliens! Their unique design was meant to represent modern British creativity and technology.

Izzy: What's It?

The 1996 Atlanta Olympics introduced Izzy, a blue, abstract character with big eyes and a wide grin. Originally called "Whatizit" (as in "What is it?"), Izzy could change shape and had stars in its eyes. While some people found Izzy confusing, kids enjoyed the playful and mysterious mascot. Izzy was the first computer-designed mascot, reflecting the rise of digital technology.

Soohorang: The Smiling White Tiger

At the 2018 PyeongChang Winter Olympics in South Korea, Soohorang, a cheerful white tiger, was the mascot. Tigers are important in Korean culture, symbolizing strength and protection. Soohorang became popular for his friendly antics and cute dance moves! Mascots often reflect the host country's culture and traditions.

Cobi: The Cubist Dog

The 1992 Barcelona Olympics featured Cobi, a sheepdog designed in a cubist art style (an art movement using geometric shapes), which means he looked like he was made of squares and triangles. At first, people weren't sure about his unusual look, but Cobi became one of the most beloved Olympic mascots ever. He represented creativity and the artistic heritage of Spain.

Unexpected Victories and Hilarious Fails: The Most Surprising Wins, Bloopers, and Memorable Mistakes

Eric "The Eel" Moussambani's Slow and Steady Swim

In the 2000 Sydney Olympics, Eric Moussambani from Equatorial Guinea had never seen an Olympic-sized pool before (that's a 50-meter-long pool—really big!). He swam the 100-meter freestyle in 1 minute and 52 seconds—more than twice the time of other swimmers. Even though he finished last, the crowd cheered him on loudly. Eric learned to swim just eight months before the Olympics, showing true Olympic spirit! His story teaches us that trying your best is more important than winning.

The Marathon Runner Who Took a Shortcut

During the 1904 St. Louis Olympics, runner Fred Lorz crossed the finish line first in the marathon. However, it was discovered that he had hitched a ride in a car for part of the race! When officials found out, he was disqualified, and Thomas Hicks, who had struggled but completed the race properly, was declared the winner. This incident highlights the importance of honesty and fair play in sports.

The Upside-Down High Jumper

In the 1968 Mexico City Olympics, American athlete Dick Fosbury introduced a new high jump technique called the "Fosbury Flop." Instead of jumping facing forward, he went over the bar backward and headfirst, landing on his back. People thought it looked odd at first, but he won the gold medal, and his style is now the standard method used by high jumpers worldwide. Sometimes, thinking differently can lead to great success!

The Marathon Runner Who Took a Nap

In the 1908 London Olympics, Italian runner Dorando Pietri entered the stadium first but was exhausted and disoriented (confused). He collapsed multiple times and even ran the wrong way! Officials helped him cross the finish line, but he was later disqualified because athletes aren't allowed assistance. His dramatic finish made him a hero, and he was awarded a special cup for his determination. This story shows how perseverance is admired, even if you don't win.

Row, Row, Row... in a Circle?

At the 1928 Amsterdam Olympics, Australian rower Henry Pearce stopped mid-race to let a family of ducks pass in front of his boat. Even with the pause, he still won the race! His kindness to the ducks made him a beloved figure and showed that good sportsmanship (being kind and fair) is more important than winning at all costs.

Olympic Myths and Mysteries: Urban Legends and Strange Occurrences from the Games

The Missing Marathon Runner

In the 1912 Stockholm Olympics, Japanese runner Shizo Kanakuri disappeared during the marathon. Feeling unwell, he dropped out of the race and quietly went home without telling officials. For over 50 years, he was considered missing! In 1967, he was invited back to finish the race, which he did with a total time of 54 years, 8 months, 6 days, 5 hours, 32 minutes, and 20.3 seconds—the longest marathon ever! It's a funny way to complete a race after so many years.

The Curse of the Olympic Gold

There's a myth that Olympic gold medals bring bad luck to some winners. For example, after winning gold, athletes might face personal challenges. But don't worry—it's just a superstition (a belief that's not based on reason or fact)! Most athletes go on to live happy and successful lives, proving that the so-called curse isn't real.

Ghost Runner of the Stadium

Some people like to tell spooky stories about old Olympic stadiums, like the one in Berlin built for the 1936 Games. They say a runner's ghost jogs around at night, but there's no evidence of ghosts—just fun tales to spark imagination! Such myths add mystery but aren't based on facts.

The Five-Second Soccer Match

A rumor once claimed that the shortest soccer match in Olympic history lasted only five seconds due to a massive brawl between teams (a big fight). In reality, no such match occurred. All official Olympic soccer matches have been played to completion, making this story an urban legend (a widely told but untrue story).

Medals Made from Recycled Electronics

Here's a strange but true fact: For the Tokyo 2020 Olympics, all the medals were made from recycled electronic devices like old smartphones and laptops. People across Japan donated millions of gadgets to extract the necessary metals. It's a cool way to recycle and make the medals even more special! This shows how the Olympics can promote caring for the environment.

Fun Finale: The Olympics' Quirky Side

The Athlete Who Won Gold in Both Summer and Winter Olympics

Eddie Eagan from the USA is the only person to win gold medals in both the Summer and Winter Olympics in different sports. He won gold in boxing in 1920 and in bobsleigh (a sport where teams race down an ice track in a sled) in 1932. What an all-around champion! Competing in such different sports shows incredible versatility.

The Swimmer Who Got a Surprise Visit

During the 2008 Beijing Olympics, a playful frog joined swimmers in the pool during a training session! The unexpected visitor made everyone laugh and showed that even frogs are fans of the Olympics. It's a funny reminder that nature can surprise us anywhere.

The Oldest Olympic Sport That Isn't a Sport

Did you know that art competitions were part of the Olympics from 1912 to 1948? Medals were awarded for artworks inspired by sports, including painting, sculpture, literature, music, and architecture. Artists were considered Olympic competitors! This idea came from the ancient Olympics, where arts and sports were both celebrated.

An Olympian with a Day Job

British athlete Ken Matthews, who won gold in race walking in 1964, returned home to his regular job as an electrician. Back then, many athletes were amateurs (they didn't get paid to play sports) who balanced sports with everyday careers. His coworkers greeted him with a cake shaped like a light bulb! This shows how athletes often had to juggle sports with regular work.

From tug-of-war champions to one-eyed mascots, the Olympics are full of wild and wacky moments. These stories show the Games aren't just about medals—they're about fun, surprises, and the joy of coming together. So next time you watch, keep an eye out for the unexpected—you never know what amazing thing might happen!

Olympic Legends

UNFORGETTABLE HEROES THAT MADE HISTORY

Perseverance and Triumph: Stories of Athletes Who Overcame Great Odds

Wilma Rudolph: From Polio to Olympic Gold

Imagine not being able to walk properly as a child and then becoming the fastest woman in the world! That's exactly what Wilma Rudolph did. Born in 1940 in Tennessee, Wilma Rudolph faced many health problems. She was the 20th of 22 siblings (that's a big family!). Born prematurely (meaning she was born too early and was very small), she weighed only 4.5 pounds (about the weight of a pineapple). At age four, she contracted a disease called polio, that can cause paralysis (trouble moving parts of your body). Doctors told her she might never walk again without braces (special supports for her legs). But Wilma was determined to walk and run like other kids. With her family's help, she did exercises every day. Her brothers and sisters took turns massaging her weak leg. By age 12, she could walk without braces or special shoes—what an achievement! She discovered she loved running and joined her school's track team. Fast forward to the 1960 Rome Olympics: Wilma won three gold medals in sprinting events—the 100 meters, 200 meters, and 4x100 meters relay. She became the first American woman to win three gold medals in track and field at a single Olympics! People called her "The Tornado" because she was so fast. Wilma's incredible journey shows that with courage and hard work, you can overcome huge obstacles and achieve your dreams.

Derek Redmond: Finishing the Race with Heart

At the 1992 Barcelona Olympics, British runner Derek Redmond had high hopes of winning a medal in the 400 meters race. He had trained for years and was one of the favorites to win. But halfway through his semi-final race, he felt a sharp pain—his hamstring muscle had torn (a serious injury in the back of the thigh). He fell to the ground, clutching his leg. Most people would have stopped, Derek was determined to finish, he stood up and began hobbling (limping) towards the finish line. Suddenly, a man ran onto the track—it was his dad! Security tried to stop him, but he insisted. He put his arm around Derek and said, "You don't have to do this." Derek replied, "Yes, I do." His dad said, "Then we're going to finish this together." The crowd of 65,000 spectators stood up, cheering and some even crying, as they watched father and son cross the finish line arm in arm. Derek didn't win a medal, but he showed the world the true meaning of perseverance and love. His story reminds us that sometimes, the biggest victories aren't about winning first place but about never giving up.

Breaking Barriers: Athletes Who Made Social and Cultural Impact

Jesse Owens: Triumph Over Prejudice

In 1936, the Olympics were held in Berlin, Germany, during a time when unfair ideas about race were widespread, especially promoted by the Nazi government, which believed in the superiority of the "Aryan race" (a false idea that some people are better because of their race). Jesse Owens, an African-American athlete from the USA, faced discrimination but didn't let that stop him. He competed in track and field events and amazed everyone by winning four gold medals in the 100 meters, 200 meters, long jump, and 4x100 meters relay. Jesse's victories proved that talent and hard work are what truly matter, not the color of your skin. He became a hero and showed the world that sports can help break down barriers between people. Even in the face of prejudice, he stood tall and proud. Jesse Owens' story teaches us about courage and the power of standing up against unfairness.

Nadia Comăneci: The Perfect 10

At the 1976 Montreal Olympics, a 14-year-old gymnast from Romania named Nadia Comăneci did something no one had ever done before. She scored a perfect 10 on the uneven bars! The scoreboard wasn't even set up to show a 10, so it displayed 1.00 instead, confusing everyone at first. Nadia went on to earn seven perfect 10s during the Games and won three gold medals. Her amazing performance changed gymnastics forever. She showed that with dedication and grace, perfection is possible. Nadia inspired countless young gymnasts around the world, proving that age is just a number when it comes to achieving greatness. She made gymnastics more popular and set new standards for excellence.

Incredible Feats: Record Breakers and the Greatest Performances in Olympic History

Florence Griffith Joyner: Redefining Speed and Style

Famously known as "Flo-Jo," Florence was a revolution on the track. Born in 1959, in the heart of Los Angeles's Watts neighborhood, she was the seventh of eleven children. Early on, her lightning speed set her apart, and with her family's enthusiastic support, she seized every chance to compete, leaving spectators in awe. Flo-Jo turned heads with her vibrant self-expression—bold, eye-catching outfits and those legendary, dramatically long, colorful fingernails that became her signature. In 1988, Flo-Jo rewrote sports history. On July 16, at the U.S. Olympic Trials, she blazed through the 100 meters in an astonishing 10.49 seconds—a world record that still defies the clock today. At the Seoul Olympics, she was unstoppable, setting a new world record in the 200 meters with a time of 21.34 seconds. She swept up three gold medals in the 100m, 200m, and 4x100m relay, and added a silver in the 4x400m relay. Her feats were seismic shifts that expanded the boundaries of human potential in athletics. After her Olympic triumphs, Flo-Jo retired from competitive running in 1989 but continued to blaze trails off the track.

She ventured into fashion design, championed public service initiatives, and promoted sports participation, including serving on the President's Council on Physical Fitness and Sports.

Fanny Blankers-Koen: The Flying Housewife

Fanny Blankers-Koen was a Dutch athlete who became a legend at the 1948 London Olympics. At 30 years old and a mother of two children, some people thought she was too old to compete and that mothers shouldn't be athletes. But Fanny proved them all wrong by winning four gold medals in track and field events: the 100 meters, 200 meters, 80-meter hurdles, and 4x100 meters relay. She tied the record for the most gold medals won by a woman at a single Olympics. She was nicknamed the "Flying Housewife" because she balanced being an athlete with taking care of her family. Fanny showed that women can be champions both on the track and at home. Her incredible feats broke barriers for female athletes and inspired women everywhere to pursue their dreams, no matter their age or responsibilities.

Heart Over Gold: Inspirational Stories of Athletes Who Didn't Win, but Made History in Other Ways

Eddie "The Eagle" Edwards: Flying with Determination

Michael "Eddie" Edwards, known as "Eddie the Eagle," was a British ski jumper who captured hearts at the 1988 Calgary Winter Olympics. Britain didn't have a ski jumping team, but Eddie was determined to compete anyway. He had thick glasses that often fogged up in the cold, and he trained without the fancy equipment other athletes had. He was also heavier than most ski jumpers, which made it harder to fly far. Eddie finished last in both of his events, but he became a fan favorite for his spirit and determination. People admired him for chasing his dream against all odds. Eddie's story reminds us that the Olympic spirit is about daring to try and giving it your all, even if you don't win.

Eric Moussambani: Swimming into Hearts

At the 2000 Sydney Olympics, Eric Moussambani from Equatorial Guinea competed in the 100 meters freestyle swimming event. He had learned to swim only eight months before the Olympics and had trained in a hotel pool that was only 13 meters long! During his race, the other swimmers were disqualified for false starts (they started before the signal), so Eric swam alone. He struggled but kept going, and the crowd cheered louder with each stroke. His time was much slower than other Olympic swimmers, but he finished the race with determination. Eric became known as "Eric the Eel" and became a symbol of perseverance, showing that it's not about where you place, but that you finish what you start. His courage inspired many people around the world.

Fun Finale: Heroes Who Inspire Us All

Usain Bolt: The Fastest Man Alive

Usain Bolt from Jamaica is known worldwide as the fastest man alive. He has won eight Olympic gold medals and holds world records in the 100 meters, 200 meters, and 4x100 meters relay. Usain's lightning speed and joyful personality made him a superstar. He loved to entertain the crowd with his famous "Lightning Bolt" pose—a fun gesture where he points to the sky. Usain showed that having fun and working hard can go together. He inspires young athletes to enjoy what they do and to run towards their dreams with a big smile. His success put a spotlight on his home country, Jamaica, inspiring pride.

Yusra Mardini: Swimming for Survival and Hope

Yusra Mardini is a swimmer from Syria who competed in the 2016 Rio Olympics as part of the Refugee Olympic Team—a team for athletes who had to leave their countries because of danger or war. Yusra and her sister fled their country because of war. During their journey across the sea, the boat they were in began to sink. Yusra, her sister, and two others jumped into the cold water and swam for over three hours, pushing the boat to safety and saving everyone's lives. At the Olympics, Yusra didn't win a medal, but she brought attention to the struggles of refugees around the world. Her courage and determination remind us that athletes are not just competitors—they can be heroes who make a real difference. She continues to inspire hope and works with the United Nations to help refugees.

From Wilma Rudolph's journey from illness to Olympic champion to Yusra Mardini's incredible bravery, these stories show the Olympics are about more than medals—they're about perseverance, courage, and chasing your dreams. These athletes overcame challenges, broke records, and inspired the world. Their stories remind us that with hard work and determination, anything is possible. Whether you're running, swimming, or dreaming big, remember: these legends were once kids like you. Maybe one day, you'll create your own unforgettable story!

Olympic Legacy

Stories That Will Live Forever!

Beyond the exciting competitions, shiny medals, and amazing ceremonies, the Olympics leave behind something even more special—a lasting legacy that touches hearts around the world. You see, the Games aren't just a two-week event; they're a global movement that keeps inspiring people long after the final race is run. One of the most wonderful things about the Olympics is how they bring peace and unity to the world. Imagine athletes from countries that might not always get along coming together to compete fairly and cheer for one another. It's a powerful reminder that, even though we're different, we're all people trying our best and sharing joyful experiences.

This spirit of togetherness doesn't just happen by chance; it's like a bridge that connects nations during tough times. For example, in the 1992 Barcelona Olympics, after big changes swept through Europe, athletes from new countries joined forces to compete as one team. This amazing collaboration showed how the Olympics can turn sports into a way for people to understand each other better and for nations to come together. When athletes shake hands or hug after a competition, it's a symbol of peace and friendship that can help ease problems between countries.

But the magic of the Olympics doesn't stop with the athletes on the field. Behind every great competitor is a team of helpers—coaches, trainers, and family members—who cheer them on every step of the way. These incredible people guide athletes, help them improve, and offer support during tough times. Coaches, especially, play a huge role. They help with training; encourage athletes to overcome challenges and believe in themselves. For many Olympians, their support team is like a second family, making their journey to greatness a shared adventure filled with hard work and joy.

As the Games unfold, something wonderful happens: the Olympics turn into a giant cultural festival. Athletes and fans from all over the world gather to learn about different cultures, languages, and traditions. Imagine an athlete who has never left their country suddenly finding themselves in the bustling Olympic Village, surrounded by new friends speaking many languages and sharing delicious foods they've never tried before. This creates an atmosphere of excitement and curiosity that brings people closer together. For those watching at home, it's like opening a window to the world, enjoying the amazing diversity without leaving their living rooms.

Throughout the years, the Olympics have been the stage for historic moments that go beyond sports. Take the 1968 Mexico City Olympics, for instance, where two American athletes, Tommie Smith and John Carlos, raised their fists during the medal ceremony to stand up against unfair treatment of people. This powerful gesture echoed around the globe and showed how athletes can use their platform to make a difference. Then there's the "Miracle on Ice" in 1980, when the U.S. men's hockey team, made up mostly of college players, beat the mighty Soviet Union team. It became a symbol of national pride and proved that with teamwork and determination, anything is possible. These moments remind us how the Olympics can shape global culture and history, inspiring generations to dream big.

But have you ever wondered what happens after the Olympic flame goes out and the athletes go home? Hosting the Games can change a city forever. Cities often build big stadiums and improve roads and buildings for the event, hoping these changes will keep helping the city long after. Ideally, these places become great sports centers or venues for future events, bringing joy to people for years to come. However, not all cities manage this well. Some Olympic venues end up unused, which shows how tricky it can be to balance the costs and benefits of hosting. On the bright side, cities like Barcelona have enjoyed more tourists and worldwide recognition because of the Games, proving that with good planning, the Olympics can leave a positive legacy that continues to benefit the community.

Another exciting development is how the Olympics are becoming more environmentally friendly. As people around the world focus on taking care of our planet, the Games are joining in this important mission. Cities like Tokyo and Paris are leading the way by building reusable facilities, reducing waste, and using renewable energy. This fits perfectly with a bigger movement toward sustainability, and the Olympic Committee wants to set a good example. By lowering the environmental impact of the Games, the Olympics are a chance to help the Earth, making sure future generations can enjoy a healthy planet.

Fair play is super important in sports, and the Olympics take it very seriously. Athletes are expected to compete honestly and follow the rules. Unfortunately, some people don't always play fair, so there are strict measures to make sure everyone is on the same playing field. The Olympic Committee and other sports organizations work hard to prevent cheating because fairness is at the heart of the Olympic spirit. While there have been problems in the past, ongoing efforts to keep competitions fair show how vital honesty is. Athletes who cheat risk losing their medals and damaging their reputations, which can be heartbreaking after years of dedication and hard work.

The Olympics have changed a lot since the first modern Games in 1896. They've added women's events, introduced new sports like skateboarding and surfing, and given more attention to the Paralympic Games. This evolution shows how the Olympics adapt over time, becoming more inclusive and diverse than ever before. Today, the Games celebrate athletes of all genders, backgrounds, and abilities, making it a truly global event where everyone has a chance to shine and share their talents with the world.

Speaking of diversity, the Paralympic Games are a shining example of courage and determination. These incredible athletes compete with amazing skill, showing that physical challenges don't limit what a person can achieve. The Paralympics have become very popular, with millions of people watching these inspiring events. From wheelchair basketball to swimming for athletes who are blind, the Paralympics showcase sports in ways that change how we think and highlight the strength of the human spirit. They remind us that with passion and perseverance, we can overcome obstacles and reach our dreams.

Looking ahead, the future of the Olympics is full of exciting possibilities. With fast technological advances, we might see new and fun ways to enjoy the Games. Imagine using virtual reality to feel like you're right there in the stadium, cheering alongside fans from all over the world. Or picture drones capturing every thrilling moment of a race live, giving us views we've never seen before. As the world becomes more connected, the spirit of the Olympics will keep growing, spreading the values of friendship, excellence, and respect on an even bigger stage. It's an exciting time to be part of this global celebration, and who knows what amazing moments await us in the years to come?

Also by Harris Baker

Discover More Stories by Harris Baker – Just Scan Below!

For partnerships or collaboration inquiries, contact me at

harrisbakerpublishing@gmail.com

www.ingramcontent.com/pod-product-compliance
Lightning Source LLC
Chambersburg PA
CBHW070634030426
42337CB00020B/4008